HOW TO BECOME A DIGITAL NOMAD: YOUR ROADMAP TO LOCATION INDEPENDENCE

First edition. September 13, 2023.

Copyright © 2023 SERGIO RIJO.

ISBN: 979-8223825678

Written by SERGIO RIJO.

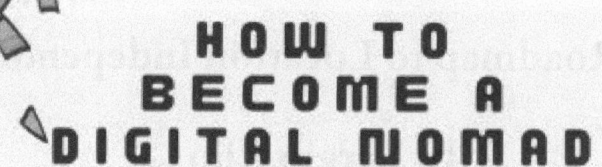

HOW TO BECOME A DIGITAL NOMAD

Your Roadmap to Location Independence

Sergio Rijo

How to Become a Digital Nomad:

Your Roadmap to Location Independence

by Sergio Rijo

Table of Contents

Chapter 1: Introduction to Digital Nomadism.................................1

Chapter 2: Assessing Your Skills and Interests............................5

Chapter 3: Setting Financial Foundations..............................10

Chapter 4: Building an Online Presence 14

Chapter 5: Remote Work Opportunities 19

Chapter 6: Location Research and Selection............................26

Chapter 7: Packing and Travel Essentials................................33

Chapter 8: Managing Your Finances Abroad 40

Chapter 9: Overcoming Common Challenges 48

Chapter 10: Maintaining Work-Life Balance......................55

Chapter 11: Networking and Building Connections 62

Chapter 12: Health and Wellness on the Road....................69

Chapter 13: Exploring New Cultures....................................76

Chapter 14: Long-Term Planning...83

Chapter 15: Environmental Responsibility 90

Chapter 16: Success Stories and Case Studies 97

Chapter 17: Legal and Regulatory Considerations.............. 103

Chapter 18: Evolving Technologies and Trends.................. 111

Chapter 19: Reflection and Personal Growth 119

Chapter 20: The Future of Digital Nomadism 126

Chapter 1: Introduction to Digital Nomadism

Hey there, fellow dreamer! Welcome to the world of digital nomadism, where the possibilities are as vast as the horizons you're about to explore. In this chapter, we're going to take a deep dive into the exciting realm of location independence, where your office can be a beach hut in Bali, a bustling café in Barcelona, or a cozy cabin in the mountains of Canada. Let's embark on this adventure together and discover what it truly means to be a digital nomad.

Defining Digital Nomadism

So, what exactly is this digital nomadism thing we keep talking about? Simply put, it's a lifestyle that allows you to break free from the confines of a traditional office job and work from anywhere with an internet connection. You become a modern-day wanderer, a digital gypsy, if you will, who thrives on the flexibility and freedom that technology brings.

Picture this: You wake up in a quaint little village nestled in the heart of Tuscany. The aroma of freshly baked bread wafts through the air as you sip your morning espresso, all while your laptop hums gently on the table. You're not on vacation; you're living this life every day. That's the essence of being a digital nomad.

But it's not just about exotic locations and envy-inducing Instagram posts. It's about crafting a life that aligns with your passions and priorities. Digital nomadism empowers you to design your own work-life balance, pursue your dreams, and experience the richness of diverse cultures.

Benefits of the Digital Nomad Lifestyle

1

Now, you might be wondering, "Why would anyone want to be a digital nomad?" Well, let me tell you, the perks are aplenty! Here are just a few of the many benefits that come with the territory:

1. Freedom

The digital nomad lifestyle is all about freedom—freedom from the 9-to-5 grind, the commute, and the limitations of a fixed location. You're the captain of your own ship, charting your course through life's adventures.

2. Adventure

Imagine having the world as your playground. With a laptop and an internet connection, you can explore new cities, cultures, and cuisines while still earning a living. It's the ultimate adventure.

3. Flexibility

No more requesting time off or feeling trapped by rigid work schedules. As a digital nomad, you decide when and where you work. Want to take a spontaneous midweek hike? Go for it. Your schedule is yours to design.

4. Personal Growth

Traveling and adapting to new environments fosters personal growth like nothing else. You'll learn to be resourceful, open-minded, and resilient as you navigate the challenges of life on the road.

5. Cost Savings

Surprisingly, living as a digital nomad can often be more cost-effective than staying in one place. You can choose destinations with a lower cost of living while maintaining your income.

6. Networking Opportunities

Digital nomad communities are thriving, both online and offline. You'll have the chance to connect with like-minded individuals, collaborate on projects, and build a diverse network of friends and colleagues.

Who Can Become a Digital Nomad?

Now that you're all fired up about the digital nomad lifestyle, you might be wondering if it's a good fit for you. Well, the beauty of it is that it's not limited to a specific age, profession, or background. Here's the thing: anyone with a desire for adventure and the willingness to adapt can become a digital nomad.

Are you a writer, a designer, a coder, a marketer, or even a teacher? Good news: many professions can be done remotely. Are you a recent college graduate eager to see the world, or perhaps a mid-career professional seeking a change of scenery? Digital nomadism doesn't discriminate based on age.

However, there are a few qualities that will serve you well on this journey:

- Adaptability

Life as a digital nomad can be unpredictable. You need to be adaptable and ready to face new challenges head-on. Embrace change and roll with the punches—it's all part of the adventure.

- Self-Motivation

With freedom comes responsibility. You'll need to be self-disciplined and motivated to meet your work commitments while resisting the temptation to binge-watch Netflix all day.

- Independence

You'll be navigating foreign cities and cultures on your own, so a degree of independence is essential. But fear not—this will also be one of the most empowering aspects of your nomadic life.

- Curiosity

Embrace your inner explorer. The digital nomad lifestyle is as much about discovering new places as it is about self-discovery. Curiosity and an open mind are your best companions.

So, there you have it—a tantalizing glimpse into the world of digital nomadism. As we journey through the following chapters, we'll dive deeper into each aspect of this thrilling lifestyle. Whether you're already packing your bags or just contemplating the idea, know that this path is open to anyone who dares to dream, explore, and redefine the boundaries of work and life. Get ready for an adventure of a lifetime!

Chapter 2: Assessing Your Skills and Interests

Alright, my fellow aspiring digital nomads, you've taken the first step by dipping your toes into the enticing waters of digital nomadism. Now, it's time to get to know yourself a little better. In this chapter, we're going to dive into the heart of the matter: assessing your skills and interests. After all, understanding yourself is key to finding the perfect remote career that will allow you to roam freely while earning a living.

Identifying Your Skills and Strengths

Let's start with a fun exercise, shall we? Picture yourself as a character in an RPG (Role-Playing Game). You've just unlocked a new skill tree, and your task is to allocate skill points. The catch? These skills aren't for slaying dragons or casting spells; they're your real-world skills, your superpowers.

Step 1: Make a Skills List

Grab a notebook or open a blank document, and start jotting down all the skills you possess. Don't be shy; this is your time to shine! Think about your work experience, hobbies, and even those random talents you've acquired over the years. Here's a little prompt to get you started:

Are you a wordsmith, wielding the power of persuasive writing?

Can you whip up a culinary masterpiece even with just a few ingredients?

Do you have the patience and precision of a watchmaker when it comes to details?

Are you a Photoshop wizard, turning ordinary images into digital art?

Are you the go-to tech guru for your friends and family?

Your list could be long or short, detailed or concise—there are no rules here. The goal is to celebrate your unique set of skills and acknowledge your strengths.

Step 2: Rate Your Skills

Now, give each skill a rating, from "Novice" to "Expert." Be honest with yourself; there's no need to inflate your abilities. This exercise is about self-awareness, not self-flattery.

Step 3: Recognize Transferable Skills

Some skills are like chameleons; they can adapt to different situations and careers. Take note of the skills that are transferable and could potentially be applied in a remote work setting. Communication, problem-solving, and time management, for example, are universally valuable.

Step 4: Identify Your Passion Projects

In addition to your professional skills, consider your hobbies and passion projects. Are there activities that you absolutely love doing, even if you're not getting paid for them? Whether it's photography, graphic design, or playing a musical instrument, these passions can become part of your remote career journey.

Exploring Your Passions and Interests

Now that you have a clearer picture of your skills and strengths, let's delve into your passions and interests. Think of this as the "what makes your heart sing" part of the equation.

Step 1: Recall Childhood Dreams

Take a trip down memory lane. What did you dream of becoming when you were a child? Sometimes, those early aspirations hold valuable clues about your true passions.

Step 2: Explore Your Hobbies

Think about how you spend your free time. Do you find yourself reading about travel destinations, experimenting with new recipes, or immersing yourself in art and culture? These interests can guide you toward a fulfilling remote career.

Step 3: List Your Dream Destinations

Imagine you have a globe in front of you, and you can choose any destination to live in for a few months. Where would you go? The answer can reveal a lot about your interests and the types of experiences that excite you.

Step 4: Seek Inspiration

Don't hesitate to seek inspiration from others. Read blogs, watch documentaries, and follow social media accounts of digital nomads who are living the life you aspire to. Their stories can ignite your own passions and help you discover new interests.

Aligning Your Skills with Potential Remote Careers

Now, let's bridge the gap between your skills and passions and the world of remote careers. The beauty of being a digital nomad is that you have a wide range of options. Here are some ideas to consider:

1. Content Creation

If you have a way with words, you can explore careers in content creation. Blogging, freelance writing, copywriting, and social media management are just a few possibilities. Your words can take you places!

2. Digital Marketing

For those with a knack for promotion and persuasion, digital marketing offers various remote opportunities. You can dive into areas like SEO, email marketing, or paid advertising.

3. Design and Multimedia

Graphic designers, photographers, and videographers can create stunning visuals that captivate online audiences. These skills are in high demand in the digital world.

4. Web Development and Programming

If you're tech-savvy, web development and programming might be your calling. Many tech-related jobs can be done remotely, from app development to cybersecurity.

5. Virtual Assistance

Organized and detail-oriented individuals can explore virtual assistant roles. You'll help others manage their tasks and schedules while working from anywhere.

6. Online Teaching and Tutoring

If you have expertise in a particular subject or language, consider teaching or tutoring online. This can be a fulfilling way to share your knowledge.

7. E-commerce and Dropshipping

Entrepreneurial spirits can start their own e-commerce businesses or venture into dropshipping. It's an exciting way to combine business acumen with adventure.

Remember, this isn't an exhaustive list. Your unique combination of skills and interests may lead you down a path that hasn't been mapped yet. The key is to keep exploring, experimenting, and staying true to your passions.

So there you have it—Chapter 2 is all about getting to know yourself, celebrating your skills, and discovering your passions. With this self-awareness, you're well on your way to finding a remote career that not only pays the bills but also fulfills your dreams.

Chapter 3: Setting Financial Foundations

Hey there, savvy future digital nomads! By now, you've embarked on a journey of self-discovery, identifying your skills, passions, and the remote career path that's calling your name. The dream is within reach, but before you pack your bags and hit the road, we need to talk about money. In this chapter, we're diving into the crucial topic of setting your financial foundations for your digital nomad adventure.

Creating a Budget for Your Digital Nomad Journey

Ah, the B-word. Budgeting might not sound as thrilling as booking a one-way ticket to Bali, but it's your compass for financial freedom as a digital nomad. Think of it as your roadmap, guiding you through the twists and turns of your newfound lifestyle.

Step 1: Calculate Your Current Expenses

Before you can create a budget for your nomadic life, you need to know where your money is going right now. Track your expenses for a few months to get a clear picture of your spending habits. Apps like Mint, YNAB (You Need a Budget), or good old-fashioned pen and paper can help.

Step 2: Determine Your Nomadic Expenses

Once you've got a handle on your current spending, it's time to estimate your future expenses as a digital nomad. Consider costs such as accommodation, transportation, food, insurance, healthcare, and entertainment. Don't forget to factor in occasional splurges and emergencies.

Step 3: Set a Realistic Budget

With your expenses in mind, create a budget that aligns with your income. Be realistic and leave room for unexpected costs. Your budget should be flexible enough to accommodate changes in your circumstances.

Step 4: Embrace Frugality

As a digital nomad, you'll quickly learn to embrace the art of frugality. Look for ways to cut unnecessary expenses and prioritize spending on experiences that truly matter to you. Remember, it's not about depriving yourself; it's about making intentional choices.

Step 5: Plan for Savings and Investments

Allocate a portion of your income to savings and investments. Building financial security is essential, even while living a nomadic lifestyle. Consider setting up automatic transfers to your savings or investment accounts to ensure consistency.

Building an Emergency Fund

Imagine this scenario: You're on a remote island, sipping coconut water, and working on your laptop when suddenly, disaster strikes—an unexpected medical expense, a laptop malfunction, or a canceled flight. This is where your emergency fund swoops in to save the day.

What is an Emergency Fund?

An emergency fund is like a financial safety net. It's a stash of cash set aside to cover unexpected expenses and emergencies. Having one is crucial for peace of mind as a digital nomad.

How Much Should You Save?

A common rule of thumb is to have three to six months' worth of living expenses saved up. This provides a cushion to handle unexpected setbacks without derailing your journey. As your income and expenses change, adjust your emergency fund accordingly.

Where to Keep Your Emergency Fund

Keep your emergency fund in a separate, easily accessible account, like a high-yield savings account. This ensures that the money is readily available when you need it.

When to Use Your Emergency Fund

Your emergency fund is for genuine emergencies, not impulse purchases or planned expenses. It's there to cover unexpected medical bills, urgent travel expenses, or unforeseen work-related costs.

Reducing Debt and Financial Obligations

Debt can be a heavy anchor when you're trying to sail the seas of digital nomadism. While it might not be possible to eliminate all your debts before you start your journey, you can take steps to minimize them and manage your financial obligations effectively.

Prioritize High-Interest Debts

Start by tackling high-interest debts like credit card balances. High-interest debt can quickly spiral out of control and eat into your budget. Make a plan to pay down these debts aggressively.

Consolidate or Refinance

Explore options to consolidate or refinance your debts at lower interest rates. This can make your debt more manageable and reduce the overall interest you pay.

Create a Debt Paydown Plan

Create a clear debt paydown plan with specific goals and timelines. Knowing when you'll be debt-free can be incredibly motivating and help you stay on track.

Minimize Fixed Expenses

As a digital nomad, minimizing fixed expenses can give you more financial flexibility. Consider downsizing your living arrangements, renegotiating contracts, or finding cost-effective alternatives for things like insurance and subscriptions.

Budget for Debt Repayment

Include debt repayment in your budget. Treat it as a non-negotiable expense to ensure you're making progress towards becoming debt-free.

Build Good Financial Habits

Ultimately, the key to reducing and managing debt is to build and maintain good financial habits. Track your expenses, stick to your budget, and avoid accumulating new debt whenever possible.

By creating a budget, building an emergency fund, and taking steps to reduce debt and financial obligations, you're laying a solid financial foundation for your digital nomad journey. This isn't about squeezing every penny; it's about securing your financial well-being so you can fully embrace the adventures that lie ahead.

Chapter 4: Building an Online Presence

Now that you've got your financial foundations in order, it's time to embark on the next exciting phase of your journey: building a robust online presence. In this digital age, your online persona is your passport to the remote work world. So, grab your metaphorical shovel because we're about to dig into the art of creating a personal brand, establishing a strong online presence, and leveraging social media for networking.

Creating a Personal Brand

First things first, let's talk about personal branding. In a world overflowing with information and digital noise, your personal brand is your unique identity—the essence of who you are and what you stand for.

1. Self-Discovery

Building a personal brand starts with self-discovery. Ask yourself these questions: What are your values? What do you love to do? What sets you apart from others? Your answers will help you shape your brand.

2. Define Your Niche

Find your niche within your chosen field or industry. It's easier to stand out when you're known for something specific. Whether you're a freelance writer specializing in travel narratives or a web developer with expertise in e-commerce, hone in on your niche.

3. Craft Your Story

Your personal brand isn't just a logo or a tagline—it's a story. Share your journey, your experiences, and your expertise. Be authentic and relatable. People connect with stories, not sterile corporate jargon.

4. Consistency is Key

Consistency is the secret sauce of personal branding. Use the same profile picture across all platforms, maintain a consistent tone in your content, and stick to your brand message.

5. Show, Don't Tell

Don't just tell people about your skills; show them. Share your work, your projects, and your successes. Let your portfolio speak for itself.

6. Be Engaging

Engage with your audience. Respond to comments, ask questions, and participate in discussions. Building a personal brand is about building relationships.

7. Authenticity Rules

Authenticity is the cornerstone of personal branding. Be yourself, and don't try to be someone you're not. Authenticity is what makes you memorable.

Establishing a Strong Online Presence

Now that you've laid the groundwork for your personal brand, it's time to establish a strong online presence. This is where the digital magic happens.

1. Build a Professional Website

Your website is your digital home. It's where people can learn more about you and your work. Include your portfolio, a blog if you like to write, and a contact page for inquiries.

2. Optimize Your LinkedIn Profile

LinkedIn is a powerful tool for professionals. Make sure your profile is complete and up to date. Connect with others in your industry and participate in relevant groups and discussions.

3. Start a Blog

If you enjoy writing, consider starting a blog. Share your insights, experiences, and expertise in your niche. A blog can establish you as a thought leader in your field.

4. Leverage Visual Platforms

Visual platforms like Instagram and Pinterest are fantastic for showcasing your work, especially if it's visually appealing. Use these platforms to tell your story through images.

5. Create Valuable Content

Whether it's blog posts, videos, podcasts, or social media updates, create content that provides value to your audience. Solve their problems, answer their questions, and share your knowledge.

6. Guest Post and Collaborate

Guest posting on reputable websites and collaborating with influencers in your industry can help you reach a wider audience and establish your expertise.

7. Monitor Your Online Reputation

Google yourself regularly to see what comes up. Address any negative information and actively manage your online reputation.

Leveraging Social Media for Networking

Social media isn't just for sharing cat memes and vacation photos (though that's fun too). It's a powerful tool for networking and connecting with like-minded individuals in your field.

1. Choose the Right Platforms

Not all social media platforms are created equal. Pick the ones that align with your personal brand and where your target audience hangs out.

2. Engage Authentically

Engage with others genuinely and authentically. Don't just promote your own stuff; share, comment, and support others in your industry.

3. Join Groups and Communities

Many platforms have groups or communities where professionals in your field gather. Join these groups to network and learn from others.

4. Use Direct Messaging Wisely

Don't be afraid to reach out to people directly. A polite, personalized message can go a long way in building relationships.

5. Attend Virtual Events

In the age of remote work, virtual events, webinars, and conferences have become the norm. Attend these events to network and learn from industry experts.

6. Give Before You Get

Networking isn't just about what you can gain—it's also about what you can give. Offer your help, expertise, or support to others without expecting anything in return.

7. Be Patient

Building meaningful connections takes time. Don't expect instant results. Be patient and consistent in your efforts.

By creating a personal brand, establishing a strong online presence, and leveraging social media for networking, you're setting yourself up for success in the digital nomad world. Remember, this journey is not just about where you're going; it's also about who you're becoming along the way. I

Chapter 5: Remote Work Opportunities

Hey there, digital nomad dreamers! Now that you've got a shiny online presence and a personal brand that's ready to dazzle, it's time to talk about the meat and potatoes of your journey: remote work opportunities. In this chapter, we're going to explore the wide world of remote job options, uncover the exciting realm of freelancing and consulting, and even dip our toes into the entrepreneurial waters of starting your own online business. Ready? Let's dive in!

Exploring Remote Job Options

Remote work opportunities are as diverse as the colors in a sunset, and they can cater to various skill sets, interests, and career goals. Let's explore some remote job options that might align with your unique journey.

1. Remote Employee

Many companies offer remote positions across various industries. Whether you're a software developer, a marketing specialist, a customer support agent, or a project manager, remote employee positions are available if you know where to look. Websites like Remote.co, We Work Remotely, and FlexJobs can help you find these opportunities.

2. Virtual Assistant

If you're detail-oriented and organized, becoming a virtual assistant might be a perfect fit. You can assist entrepreneurs, executives, or small business owners with tasks like email management, scheduling, and administrative work.

3. Content Creator

Writers, designers, videographers, and photographers can thrive in the world of content creation. You can work as a freelance content creator, contributing to blogs, websites, social media, and more.

4. Online Teaching and Tutoring

If you have expertise in a subject or language, consider teaching or tutoring online. Platforms like VIPKID, Teachable, and Udemy allow you to share your knowledge with students around the world.

5. E-commerce and Dropshipping

Entrepreneurial spirits can explore e-commerce and dropshipping. You can start your own online store, source products, and manage your business remotely.

6. Remote Sales and Marketing

Sales and marketing professionals often have the flexibility to work remotely. You can find remote positions in areas like digital marketing, sales development, and account management.

7. IT and Tech Support

Technical skills are in high demand, and many IT and tech support roles can be done remotely. You can troubleshoot issues, provide customer support, or even work as a remote systems administrator.

8. Data Entry and Online Research

If you have strong attention to detail, data entry and online research jobs are available. These roles often involve gathering information, analyzing data, and maintaining databases.

9. Translation and Language Services

Bilingual or multilingual individuals can work as translators, interpreters, or language specialists. You can help bridge language gaps in various industries.

10. Project Management

Experienced project managers can oversee remote teams and coordinate projects from anywhere. This role is essential for keeping remote work on track.

11. Remote Healthcare and Telemedicine

Healthcare professionals, including doctors, therapists, and nurses, can provide remote healthcare services through telemedicine platforms.

Remember, the remote work landscape is continually evolving. New opportunities emerge as technology advances and industries adapt to the digital age. Keep an open mind and stay updated on trends in your field to maximize your chances of finding the perfect remote job.

Freelancing and Consulting Opportunities

Now, let's dive into the exhilarating world of freelancing and consulting. These paths offer even more flexibility and autonomy in your remote work journey.

Freelancing

Freelancing means working as an independent contractor, offering your services to clients on a project basis. It's a fantastic way to tailor your work to your skills and interests. Here's how to get started:

1. Identify Your Niche

Determine your niche or specialty. What services can you offer that are in demand? Your personal brand can play a significant role here,

21

as clients are more likely to hire someone with a clear and compelling brand.

2. Create a Portfolio

As a freelancer, your portfolio is your resume. Showcase your best work, highlight your skills, and demonstrate what you can bring to the table. Visuals, testimonials, and case studies can all bolster your portfolio.

3. Set Your Rates

Determining your rates can be a bit tricky. Research what others in your niche are charging, but also consider your experience, expertise, and the value you provide. It's okay to start lower and gradually increase your rates as you gain experience.

4. Find Clients

There are various platforms where you can find freelance work, such as Upwork, Freelancer, and Fiverr. Networking, referrals, and pitching to potential clients can also help you secure projects.

Consulting

Consulting takes freelancing to the next level. As a consultant, you're seen as an expert in your field, and clients seek your advice and guidance. Here's how to make the leap to consulting:

1. Establish Expertise

To become a consultant, you must be seen as an authority in your niche. Publish articles, give talks, and build a strong online presence to showcase your expertise.

2. Define Your Services

Clearly define the services you offer as a consultant. This might include strategy development, problem-solving, and advising clients on specific challenges.

3. Build a Network

Networking is vital in consulting. Connect with professionals in your field, attend industry events, and actively seek out opportunities to collaborate.

4. Offer Solutions

Consulting is all about providing solutions. Clients hire you to help them overcome obstacles, improve processes, or achieve their goals. Your ability to deliver results is your most valuable asset.

5. Marketing and Branding

As a consultant, your personal brand is critical. Craft a professional image, develop a compelling brand message, and market your services effectively.

6. Pricing Your Consulting Services

Consulting rates can vary widely, depending on your niche and experience. It's common to charge by the hour, day, or project. Just like with freelancing, research industry standards and adjust your rates accordingly.

Starting Your Own Online Business

For the bold and entrepreneurial among us, starting your own online business is the ultimate adventure. It's a path that offers unlimited potential for creativity, innovation, and financial success. Here's how to get started:

1. Find Your Business Idea

Start by identifying a business idea that aligns with your skills, passions, and market demand. What problem can you solve or need can you fulfill?

2. Market Research

Conduct thorough market research to validate your business idea. Who are your competitors? Is there demand for your product or service? What's your unique value proposition?

3. Business Plan

Create a comprehensive business plan that outlines your business goals, target audience, marketing strategy, financial projections, and operational plan. A solid plan is your roadmap to success.

4. Legal Considerations

Register your business and ensure compliance with local and international regulations. This may include obtaining the necessary licenses and permits.

5. Build Your Online Presence

Your website is the heart of your online business. Invest in professional web design, and optimize your site for search engines (SEO) to attract organic traffic.

6. Marketing and Sales

Develop a marketing strategy to promote your business. Use social media, content marketing, email marketing, and online advertising to reach your target audience.

7. Customer Service and Support

Deliver exceptional customer service to build trust and loyalty. Happy customers can become your biggest advocates.

8. Adapt and Evolve

The business landscape is constantly changing. Be prepared to adapt, innovate, and evolve your business to stay competitive and relevant.

Starting your own online business can be challenging, but the rewards are immense. It's an opportunity to shape your destiny and create something meaningful.

So, there you have it—remote work opportunities, freelancing and consulting, and the thrilling world of starting your own online business. Your journey as a digital nomad is as unique as your fingerprint, and these options provide a spectrum of possibilities to craft the life you've been dreaming of.

Chapter 6: Location Research and Selection

Hey there, future globe-trotter! You've built the foundations, fine-tuned your online presence, and explored various remote work opportunities. Now, it's time to pick the stage for your next adventure: the destination. In this chapter, we're diving deep into location research and selection, where we'll explore the factors to consider when choosing a destination, delve into the nitty-gritty of visa and immigration requirements, and discover the treasure trove of digital nomad-friendly communities waiting to welcome you.

Factors to Consider When Choosing a Destination

Choosing the right destination as a digital nomad is like picking the perfect flavor of ice cream—there's no one-size-fits-all answer. It depends on your preferences, lifestyle, and career. Let's explore the key factors to consider:

1. Cost of Living

Different destinations come with varying price tags. Research the cost of living in your potential destinations, considering accommodation, food, transportation, and leisure activities. Consider places where your budget aligns comfortably.

2. Visa and Immigration Regulations

Visa regulations can be complex and vary widely between countries. Consider destinations that offer favorable visa options for digital nomads. Some countries have specific digital nomad visas, while others offer extended tourist visas or visa-free stays.

3. Internet Connectivity

A strong and reliable internet connection is non-negotiable for remote work. Research the quality and availability of internet services in your chosen destination. Look for co-working spaces and cafes with high-speed internet as backup options.

4. Time Zone Compatibility

If your remote job involves regular meetings or collaboration with teams in specific time zones, choose a destination that aligns with your work hours. Being on the other side of the world can lead to sleepless nights and groggy mornings.

5. Safety and Security

Safety is paramount when traveling. Check travel advisories, research local safety conditions, and read reviews from other travelers to gauge the safety of your chosen destination.

6. Healthcare Facilities

Access to quality healthcare is essential, especially if you're traveling long-term. Research the availability of hospitals, clinics, and health insurance options in your destination.

7. Language and Culture

Consider your language skills and cultural preferences. Are you comfortable in a destination where you don't speak the language, or do you thrive in cultural immersion? The language and culture of your chosen destination can greatly impact your experience.

8. Climate and Weather

Climate can influence your lifestyle and activities. Do you prefer sunny beaches, snowy mountains, or temperate cities? Your destination's climate can play a significant role in your overall happiness.

9. Community and Networking Opportunities

Digital nomad-friendly communities can provide support, networking opportunities, and a sense of belonging. Research whether your chosen destination has an active digital nomad community.

10. Personal Interests and Hobbies

Consider your personal interests and hobbies. If you love surfing, you might want to head to a coastal destination. If you're a history buff, a city with rich historical sites might be your ideal spot.

11. Travel Goals

Think about your travel goals and aspirations. Do you want to explore multiple destinations, settle down in one place for a while, or follow a specific travel itinerary? Your travel goals will shape your destination choices.

12. Nomad Friendliness

Some destinations are more welcoming to digital nomads than others. Research whether your chosen location has the infrastructure and amenities that cater to remote workers, such as co-working spaces and affordable accommodation.

Researching Visa and Immigration Requirements

Visa and immigration requirements can be the gateway—or roadblock—to your digital nomad adventure. Let's navigate this sometimes complex landscape together:

1. Understand Your Citizenship

Your passport's country of issuance determines your visa and immigration options. Research the visa-free or visa-on-arrival countries available to your nationality.

2. Explore Digital Nomad Visas

Some countries have recognized the growing trend of digital nomadism and introduced specific visas for remote workers. These visas often come with fewer restrictions than traditional work visas.

3. Check Visa Duration

Examine the duration of the visa or stay permitted in your chosen destination. Some visas may allow you to stay for a few months, while others offer longer-term options.

4. Visa Application Process

Research the visa application process for your destination. Determine whether you can apply online, at an embassy or consulate, or upon arrival. Be prepared to gather the required documents, including proof of income and health insurance.

5. Financial Requirements

Some countries may require proof of sufficient funds to cover your stay. Ensure you meet the financial requirements specified by the immigration authorities.

6. Health Insurance

Health insurance is often a visa requirement. Find out if you need to purchase local health insurance or if your existing policy covers you abroad.

7. Departure Plans

Certain visas may require proof of departure, such as a return ticket or onward travel plans. Make sure you have the necessary documentation.

8. Visa Extensions

Investigate whether you can extend your visa if you decide to stay longer. Knowing your options in advance can save you from last-minute visa runs or complications.

9. Local Immigration Laws

Stay informed about the immigration laws and regulations of your chosen destination. Familiarize yourself with any restrictions on work, volunteering, or other activities you plan to engage in.

10. Seek Expert Advice

When in doubt, seek advice from fellow digital nomads, expatriate forums, or immigration experts who specialize in your destination. They can provide valuable insights and guidance.

Finding Digital Nomad-Friendly Communities

Being a digital nomad doesn't mean you have to go it alone. There are vibrant communities of like-minded individuals around the world, ready to welcome you with open arms. Here's how to find and connect with them:

1. Online Communities

Join online communities and forums dedicated to digital nomads. Facebook groups, Reddit threads, and websites like Nomad List and Digital Nomad Forum are excellent places to start.

2. Attend Co-Working Spaces

Many destinations popular among digital nomads have co-working spaces where you can work alongside others in a collaborative environment. These spaces often host networking events and workshops.

3. Nomad-Friendly Destinations

Research destinations known for their digital nomad-friendly atmosphere. Locations like Bali, Chiang Mai, Lisbon, and Tbilisi have established communities of remote workers.

4. Attend Meetups and Events

Keep an eye out for digital nomad meetups, events, and conferences happening in your chosen destination. Attending these gatherings is an excellent way to connect with fellow nomads.

5. Use Social Media

Leverage social media platforms like Instagram, Twitter, and LinkedIn to connect with other digital nomads in your destination. Don't be shy—reach out, ask questions, and arrange meetups.

6. Local Expat Groups

Many destinations have expat communities that welcome digital nomads. Seek out local expat groups or associations for social events and networking opportunities.

7. Be Open and Approachable

Approachability goes a long way in building connections. Be open to meeting new people, sharing your experiences, and learning from others.

8. Collaborate and Share

Collaborate with fellow digital nomads on projects or initiatives. Sharing your skills and knowledge can lead to meaningful relationships.

9. Create Your Own Events

If you can't find digital nomad events in your area, consider organizing your own. Host a meetup or workshop and invite others to join.

10. Build a Support Network

Building a support network of fellow digital nomads can provide a sense of community, a safety net when facing challenges, and lasting friendships.

Remember, digital nomad communities are diverse and inclusive, comprising people from all walks of life. Embrace the opportunity to learn from others, share your journey, and make connections that can last a lifetime.

With careful consideration of destination factors, diligent research into visa and immigration requirements, and a willingness to connect with digital nomad communities, you're well on your way to selecting the perfect location for your adventure.

Chapter 7: Packing and Travel Essentials

The time has come to dive into one of the most exciting (and sometimes anxiety-inducing) aspects of the digital nomad life: packing and travel essentials. In this chapter, we'll explore minimalist packing tips to help you travel light and nimble, uncover the essential travel gear and technology that will make your journey smoother, and discuss critical health and safety considerations for your nomadic lifestyle. So, grab your suitcase and let's get started on the road to packing perfection!

Minimalist Packing Tips

Packing as a digital nomad is an art form, and the mantra here is "less is more." Traveling light not only makes life on the road more manageable but also liberates you from the burden of lugging around excess baggage. Here are some minimalist packing tips to help you master the art:

1. Create a Packing List

Begin with a detailed packing list. Write down everything you think you'll need, and then go back and ruthlessly trim it down. Remember, you can buy most things on the road if you really need them.

2. Versatile Wardrobe

Opt for versatile clothing that can mix and match. Stick to a color scheme so that everything in your wardrobe goes together. Layers are your best friend—think lightweight sweaters and jackets for various weather conditions.

3. Laundry Options

Plan for laundry along the way. You don't need weeks' worth of clothes; a week's worth that you can wash is plenty. Invest in quick-dry and moisture-wicking fabrics.

4. Packing Cubes

Packing cubes are your secret weapon for keeping your luggage organized. They help maximize space and keep your belongings neat and tidy.

5. Shoes Matter

Shoes can be bulky and heavy, so choose wisely. A comfortable pair for walking, a versatile pair for dressier occasions, and perhaps a pair of flip-flops for the beach should cover your bases.

6. Tech Essentials

Pack your tech essentials efficiently. A laptop, smartphone, chargers, and any necessary adapters are a must. Consider a portable charger or power bank for those times when outlets are scarce.

7. Go Digital

Digitize your documents. Scan important documents like passports, visas, and travel insurance policies. Store them securely in the cloud so you can access them from anywhere.

8. Minimal Toiletries

You can buy toiletries at your destination, so don't overpack. Opt for travel-sized containers or reusable silicone bottles to carry your essentials.

9. Quality Backpack or Suitcase

Invest in a durable, high-quality backpack or suitcase. It's your constant companion, so choose one that suits your travel style and comfort.

10. Leave Room for Souvenirs

Remember that you might want to pick up souvenirs along the way. Leave some space in your luggage for those unique treasures you'll find during your travels.

11. Practice Packing

Before you set off on your adventure, practice packing and unpacking your bag. This will help you refine your packing process and identify any unnecessary items.

12. Embrace Minimalism

Embrace the minimalist mindset. The less you carry, the lighter you'll feel, both physically and mentally. You'll also find that fewer possessions can lead to a richer travel experience.

Essential Travel Gear and Technology

Now that you've trimmed down your packing list, let's dive into the essential travel gear and technology that will make your life on the road more comfortable and productive:

1. Travel Backpack or Suitcase

Your choice of luggage is crucial. A durable and well-designed backpack or suitcase is worth the investment.

2. Travel-Friendly Laptop

Invest in a lightweight and powerful laptop. Consider models known for their portability and long battery life.

3. Noise-Canceling Headphones

Noise-canceling headphones are a game-changer, especially when you're working in bustling cafes or dealing with noisy neighbors.

4. Travel Adapters and Power Banks

Ensure you have the right adapters for the countries you'll be visiting. A portable power bank can be a lifesaver when you're on the move.

5. Universal Travel Insurance

Travel insurance is non-negotiable. It provides peace of mind and financial protection in case of emergencies.

6. Portable Wi-Fi Hotspot

A portable Wi-Fi hotspot ensures you stay connected even in remote areas with spotty or expensive internet.

7. VPN (Virtual Private Network)

A VPN protects your online privacy and allows you to access geo-restricted content while traveling.

8. External Hard Drive or Cloud Storage

Backup your important files to an external hard drive or cloud storage. Losing your work or travel photos can be a nightmare.

9. Travel-Friendly Camera

Capture your adventures with a lightweight and versatile travel camera. Many smartphones also offer excellent camera capabilities.

10. Travel-Sized Toiletries

Pack travel-sized toiletries and consider solid or multi-use products to save space.

11. First-Aid Kit

A basic first-aid kit with essentials like band-aids, pain relievers, and antiseptic wipes can be a lifesaver in unexpected situations.

12. Travel Pillow and Eye Mask

Long journeys can be exhausting. A comfortable travel pillow and eye mask can make a big difference in getting quality rest.

13. Reusable Water Bottle

Stay hydrated while reducing plastic waste by carrying a reusable water bottle.

14. Travel Apps

Download essential travel apps for navigation, language translation, currency conversion, and local recommendations.

15. Travel Journal

A travel journal can be a cherished keepsake, allowing you to document your adventures, thoughts, and reflections.

Health and Safety Considerations

While exploring the world as a digital nomad is incredibly rewarding, it's essential to prioritize your health and safety. Here are some health and safety considerations to keep in mind:

1. Travel Insurance

We can't stress this enough: get comprehensive travel insurance that covers medical emergencies, trip cancellations, and theft. It's your safety net.

2. Vaccinations and Health Precautions

Research the vaccination requirements and health precautions for your destination. Consult a travel clinic or your healthcare provider to ensure you're up to date on necessary shots.

3. Medications and Prescriptions

Carry a sufficient supply of any prescribed medications you need. Keep them in their original containers with clear labels.

4. Travel Health Kit

Pack a small travel health kit with essentials like pain relievers, antidiarrheal medication, insect repellent, and sunscreen.

5. Emergency Contact Information

Have a list of emergency contacts, including family members, friends, and your country's embassy or consulate in your destination.

6. Stay Informed

Stay informed about local health advisories and safety tips. Keep an eye on news updates and be aware of any political or natural events in your area.

7. Personal Safety

Practice personal safety precautions, such as avoiding risky areas, securing your belongings, and being cautious when meeting new people.

8. Digital Security

Protect your digital security by using secure Wi-Fi connections, avoiding public computers for sensitive tasks, and regularly updating your passwords.

9. Emergency Funds

Always have a backup source of funds, such as a credit card or emergency cash, in case your wallet is lost or stolen.

10. Local Laws and Customs

Research the local laws and customs of your destination to avoid unintentional offenses.

11. Stay Hydrated and Well-Rested

Maintain good health by staying hydrated, eating well, and getting enough rest. Travel can be exhausting, so listen to your body.

12. Trust Your Instincts

Your intuition is a powerful tool. If something doesn't feel right, trust your instincts and take precautions.

Remember, staying healthy and safe is the foundation of an enjoyable and successful digital nomad lifestyle. With the right packing strategies, essential travel gear and technology, and a focus on health and safety, you're well-prepared for the adventures that lie ahead.

Chapter 8: Managing Your Finances Abroad

Now that you've got your bags packed, your tech gadgets charged, and your adventurous spirit roaring, it's time to tackle a crucial aspect of the digital nomad lifestyle: managing your finances abroad. In this chapter, we're going to dive into the world of banking and currency exchange options, master the art of budgeting while on the move, and demystify the tax considerations that come with being a digital nomad. So, grab your notepad and calculator, because we're about to make your financial journey smoother than a tropical breeze.

Banking and Currency Exchange Options

Navigating the financial landscape as a digital nomad can be as exhilarating as exploring a new city. Let's start by exploring your banking and currency exchange options to ensure you can access and manage your money seamlessly:

1. International Bank Accounts

Many banks offer international accounts designed for travelers. These accounts often come with low foreign transaction fees, free international ATM withdrawals, and currency exchange services. Research your home country's banks to find out if they offer such accounts.

2. Local Bank Accounts

Opening a local bank account in your destination can be advantageous. It allows you to receive payments in the local currency and save on international transaction fees. However, some countries have strict requirements for opening accounts as a foreigner, so check the regulations in advance.

3. Digital Banks

Digital or online banks are increasingly popular among digital nomads. They offer easy access to your money and often have low or no fees for international transactions. Popular options include N26, TransferWise (now called Wise), and Revolut.

4. Prepaid Travel Cards

Prepaid travel cards are a convenient way to manage your finances while abroad. They allow you to load money onto the card and use it like a debit or credit card. Look for cards with competitive exchange rates and low fees.

5. Mobile Payment Apps

In some countries, mobile payment apps like PayPal, Venmo, and Alipay are widely accepted. These apps can be a convenient way to pay for goods and services, transfer money, and even receive payments from clients.

6. Currency Exchange Apps

Currency exchange apps like Wise (formerly TransferWise) and Revolut offer competitive exchange rates and allow you to hold multiple currencies in one account. They are excellent for minimizing currency conversion costs.

7. Avoid Airport Currency Exchange

Airport currency exchange counters often offer poor exchange rates and high fees. It's usually best to avoid them and exchange money at a local bank or ATM in your destination.

8. Notify Your Bank

Before you embark on your journey, notify your bank of your travel plans. This can prevent your accounts from being flagged for suspicious activity when you use your cards abroad.

9. Emergency Funds

Always have a backup source of funds, such as a credit card or emergency cash, in case your primary payment methods fail.

10. Online Banking Security

Ensure your online banking is secure with strong passwords, two-factor authentication, and regular monitoring of your accounts. Protect your financial data as diligently as you protect your passport.

11. Keep Records

Keep detailed records of your financial transactions and expenses. This will be invaluable for budgeting and tax purposes.

12. Nomad-Friendly Banks

Some banks are known for being nomad-friendly, with features tailored to the digital nomad lifestyle. Research these options to see if they align with your needs.

Budgeting While Traveling

Ah, budgeting—the compass that keeps your financial ship on course during your nomadic adventures. Let's explore some essential budgeting strategies to ensure you make the most of your funds while on the move:

1. Create a Travel Budget

Before you even step out the door, create a travel budget. Estimate your income, expenses, and savings goals for your journey. Factor in costs like accommodation, transportation, food, activities, and emergencies.

2. Emergency Fund

Your emergency fund is your financial safety net. Aim to have at least three to six months' worth of living expenses saved up in case of unexpected events like medical emergencies or job loss.

3. Daily Spending Limit

Establish a daily spending limit to help you stay on track. Divide your monthly budget by the number of days you'll be traveling, and aim to spend within that limit.

4. Track Your Expenses

Use budgeting apps or spreadsheets to track your expenses. Categorize your spending to identify areas where you can cut back or optimize.

5. Separate Business and Personal Expenses

If you're a freelancer or remote worker, it's essential to separate your business and personal expenses. This makes accounting and tax reporting much easier.

6. Save for Taxes

As a digital nomad, you may have tax obligations both in your home country and your destination. Set aside a portion of your income for taxes to avoid surprises when tax season rolls around.

7. Automate Savings

Automate your savings by setting up recurring transfers to your emergency fund, retirement account, or other savings goals.

8. Be Frugal

Embrace a frugal mindset. Look for ways to save money without sacrificing experiences. Cook your meals occasionally, use public transportation, and seek out free or low-cost activities.

9. Avoid Impulse Purchases

Think twice before making impulse purchases. Give yourself a cooling-off period to decide if a purchase is necessary.

10. Monitor Currency Exchange Rates

Keep an eye on currency exchange rates, especially if you're dealing with multiple currencies. Timing your exchanges can save you money.

11. Use Cash Sparingly

Carrying cash can be handy, but use it sparingly. Credit cards and digital payment methods often offer better security and lower fees.

12. Review and Adjust

Regularly review your budget and spending habits. Adjust your budget as needed to reflect changes in your income or expenses.

13. Build Travel Rewards

Consider using travel rewards credit cards to earn points or miles on your expenses. These rewards can offset travel costs in the future.

14. Plan for Big Expenses

Anticipate significant expenses like flights or visa renewals and budget for them in advance.

15. Be Flexible

While having a budget is essential, it's also crucial to be flexible. Unexpected opportunities or challenges may arise, and your budget should adapt accordingly.

16. Set Financial Goals

Set specific financial goals for your journey, whether it's saving for a dream vacation or building an emergency fund. Having goals gives your finances purpose and motivation.

17. Seek Financial Advice

If you're uncertain about budgeting or financial planning, consider seeking advice from a financial advisor or consultant who specializes in working with digital nomads.

Tax Considerations for Digital Nomads

Taxes—often a word that brings a shiver down one's spine. But fear not, because understanding the tax considerations for digital nomads is essential for a worry-free journey:

1. Tax Residency

Your tax residency status can significantly impact your tax obligations. It's generally based on the amount of time you spend in a particular country and your ties to that country. Keep track of your days spent in each location.

2. Home Country Taxes

You may still be liable for taxes in your home country, even if you're living and working abroad. Research the tax laws in your home country to understand your obligations.

3. Double Taxation Agreements

Many countries have double taxation agreements to prevent you from being taxed twice on the same income. Familiarize yourself with these agreements between your home country and your destination.

4. Digital Nomad Visas

Some countries offer digital nomad visas that may come with tax benefits or exemptions. Check if your destination offers such a visa and understand the tax implications.

5. Foreign Earned Income Exclusion

In the United States, for example, the Foreign Earned Income Exclusion (FEIE) allows eligible expatriates to exclude a portion of their foreign-earned income from federal taxation. Research whether your home country has similar provisions.

6. Keep Meticulous Records

Maintain meticulous records of your income, expenses, and travel history. This documentation will be invaluable for tax reporting.

7. Consult a Tax Professional

Tax laws can be complex, especially for digital nomads. Consider consulting a tax professional who specializes in international tax issues to ensure you comply with all regulations.

8. Plan Ahead

Plan your travels with tax considerations in mind. Timing your visits to countries with favorable tax conditions can be advantageous.

9. Report Your Income

Even if you're not required to pay taxes in your destination, you may still need to report your income. Failure to do so can lead to legal issues in some countries.

10. Penalties for Non-Compliance

Be aware that penalties for tax non-compliance can be severe. It's in your best interest to be proactive and informed.

Managing your finances as a digital nomad requires diligence, organization, and a willingness to adapt to the unique financial landscape of a nomadic lifestyle. By exploring banking and currency exchange options, mastering the art of budgeting, and understanding the tax considerations, you'll navigate the financial world with confidence and focus on what truly matters—unforgettable experiences and personal growth.

Chapter 9: Overcoming Common Challenges

As a digital nomad, you're embarking on a thrilling journey filled with unforgettable experiences, but it's not all smooth sailing. In this chapter, we're going to dive into the deep waters of common challenges that digital nomads often face and equip you with the tools to overcome them. From battling loneliness and isolation to navigating time zones and communication hurdles, and gracefully handling cultural differences, we'll help you navigate the seas of nomadic life with confidence and resilience. So, grab your compass, and let's set sail into uncharted waters!

Dealing with Loneliness and Isolation

Loneliness, like a ghost ship on the horizon, can creep up on even the most seasoned digital nomad. While the freedom of traveling solo is liberating, it can also lead to moments of solitude that may feel overwhelming. Here's how to navigate these waters:

1. Build a Support System

Foster connections with fellow digital nomads, locals, and expats in your destination. Join local events, co-working spaces, and online communities to meet like-minded individuals.

2. Stay Connected with Loved Ones

Maintain regular contact with friends and family back home through video calls, messaging apps, and social media. Sharing your experiences can alleviate feelings of isolation.

3. Embrace Solitude

Loneliness can be an opportunity for self-discovery and introspection. Embrace moments of solitude to reflect, set goals, and recharge.

4. Pursue Hobbies and Interests

Engage in activities you're passionate about. Whether it's joining a local sports club, taking a cooking class, or practicing a new language, pursuing your interests can lead to fulfilling social connections.

5. Volunteer or Give Back

Giving back to the community you're in can provide a sense of purpose and connection. Look for volunteer opportunities or ways to support local causes.

6. Seek Professional Help

If loneliness persists and affects your mental health, consider seeking the help of a mental health professional or therapist, even if it's through online sessions.

7. Embrace Digital Nomad Retreats

Participating in digital nomad retreats or co-living experiences can provide a sense of community and combat loneliness.

8. Create a Routine

Establishing a daily routine can give your life structure and purpose. It can be as simple as a morning yoga session, a daily journaling practice, or a regular coffee shop visit.

9. Practice Self-Care

Prioritize self-care to maintain your mental and emotional well-being. Exercise regularly, get enough sleep, and eat nutritious meals to stay physically healthy.

10. Be Patient

Remember that loneliness is a common part of the human experience, and it's okay to feel this way at times. Be patient with yourself and allow the feeling to pass.

Time Zone and Communication Challenges

Navigating time zones and communication hurdles is a bit like steering through a digital storm. It can be challenging but not impossible. Let's explore how to keep your ship afloat:

1. Set Clear Communication Expectations

When working with clients or teams in different time zones, establish clear communication expectations. Let them know your working hours and response times.

2. Use Time Zone Converters

Time zone converter apps or websites can help you keep track of time differences and schedule meetings accordingly.

3. Leverage Scheduling Tools

Consider using scheduling tools like Calendly or Doodle to simplify the process of setting up meetings with participants in various time zones.

4. Flexible Work Hours

If your job allows it, negotiate flexible work hours that align with your preferred time zone. This can reduce the stress of constantly adjusting your schedule.

5. Embrace Asynchronous Communication

Use asynchronous communication tools like email, project management software, and messaging apps to communicate without the need for real-time responses.

6. Buffer Time for Meetings

When scheduling meetings with participants in different time zones, add a buffer time to accommodate potential delays or scheduling conflicts.

7. Prioritize Sleep and Work-Life Balance

Avoid sacrificing sleep or work-life balance to accommodate different time zones. Prioritize your well-being and communicate your boundaries to clients or colleagues.

8. Travel Strategically

Plan your travel itinerary with time zones in mind. Minimize rapid changes in time zones to reduce jet lag and adjustment stress.

9. Multinational SIM Cards

Consider using a multinational SIM card that works in multiple countries to maintain consistent mobile communication.

10. Patience and Flexibility

Practice patience and flexibility when dealing with time zone challenges. It's a part of the digital nomad lifestyle, and adaptability is your superpower.

Coping with Cultural Differences

As you traverse the globe, you'll encounter diverse cultures and customs. While this is one of the joys of nomadic life, it can also lead to moments of cultural confusion or discomfort. Here's how to navigate the cultural seas with grace:

1. Educate Yourself

Before arriving in a new destination, research its culture, customs, and etiquette. Understanding the local way of life can help you navigate with respect.

2. Be Observant

Observe how locals behave in different situations and follow their lead when uncertain about what to do.

3. Learn Basic Phrases

Learning a few basic phrases in the local language can go a long way in building rapport and showing respect.

4. Be Open-Minded

Approach new cultural experiences with an open mind and a willingness to learn. Embrace the differences rather than judge them.

5. Respect Local Customs

Respect local customs, traditions, and social norms, even if they differ from your own. This includes dress codes, greetings, and gestures.

6. Ask Questions

If you're unsure about something, don't hesitate to ask locals for guidance or clarification. Most people appreciate your interest in their culture.

7. Practice Cultural Sensitivity

Be sensitive to cultural nuances and avoid making assumptions or generalizations about a culture or its people.

8. Adapt to Local Cuisine

Try local cuisine and be open to new flavors and dishes. Food is often a gateway to understanding a culture.

9. Seek Cultural Experiences

Participate in cultural activities, festivals, and events to immerse yourself in the local culture and gain a deeper appreciation for it.

10. Show Gratitude

Express gratitude and appreciation for the hospitality and kindness you encounter along your journey.

11. Embrace Your Cultural Identity

While adapting to new cultures, don't forget to embrace your own cultural identity. Share your traditions and experiences with others.

12. Stay Safe

Prioritize your safety and well-being in unfamiliar cultural settings. Be cautious and avoid risky situations.

Cultural differences are a rich tapestry that makes travel exciting, but they can also present challenges. By approaching new cultures with respect, curiosity, and an open heart, you'll not only overcome challenges but also forge meaningful connections and enrich your nomadic journey.

Remember, every challenge you encounter is an opportunity for growth, learning, and self-discovery. By addressing these common challenges head-on, you'll become a more resilient and adaptable digital nomad, ready to conquer the world, one cultural encounter at a time.

Chapter 10: Maintaining Work-Life Balance

As a digital nomad, you're dancing to the rhythm of the world, juggling work and exploration in a delicate balance. In this chapter, we'll dive into the art of maintaining a harmonious work-life balance while navigating the nomadic life. We'll explore strategies for setting boundaries, time management techniques that keep your ship sailing smoothly, and ways to stay productive on the road. So, grab your captain's hat, and let's chart a course for work-life equilibrium!

Strategies for Setting Boundaries

When you're living and working in the same space, setting boundaries becomes paramount. Without them, you risk burning out or blurring the lines between work and leisure. Here's how to set effective boundaries:

1. Define Your Workspace

Designate a specific area for work in your accommodation. Even if it's just a corner of a room, having a dedicated workspace helps create a mental separation between work and leisure.

2. Set Clear Work Hours

Establish clear work hours that align with your productivity peaks and personal life. Communicate these hours to clients, colleagues, and yourself.

3. Create a Daily Routine

Craft a daily routine that incorporates work, leisure, exercise, and relaxation. A structured routine provides a sense of stability and ensures you make time for yourself.

4. Avoid Overworking

Resist the temptation to work around the clock. Set a limit on your daily working hours and stick to it. Overworking can lead to burnout and decreased productivity.

5. Schedule Breaks

Incorporate regular breaks into your workday. Short breaks help you recharge and maintain focus. Use techniques like the Pomodoro method to structure your work time.

6. Silence Notifications

Turn off non-essential notifications during your off-hours. This includes email alerts, work-related apps, and social media. Give yourself permission to disconnect.

7. Learn to Say No

Don't overcommit to work projects or social invitations. Be selective about the projects you take on and the events you attend to maintain a healthy balance.

8. Communicate Boundaries

Clearly communicate your boundaries to clients, colleagues, and friends. Let them know when you're available for work or social activities.

9. Set Digital Detox Days

Designate specific days for digital detox—no work, no screens. Use these days to unwind, explore, and connect with the world around you.

10. Prioritize Self-Care

Make self-care a non-negotiable part of your routine. Whether it's exercise, meditation, or a spa day, prioritize activities that rejuvenate your mind and body.

Time Management Techniques

Time is your most precious resource as a digital nomad. Mastering time management techniques can make the difference between a chaotic journey and a well-organized adventure:

1. Prioritize Tasks

Start each day by identifying your most important tasks. Use the Eisenhower Matrix to distinguish between urgent and important tasks.

2. Create a To-Do List

Maintain a to-do list that outlines your daily, weekly, and monthly tasks. Apps like Todoist or Trello can help you stay organized.

3. Set SMART Goals

Set Specific, Measurable, Achievable, Relevant, and Time-bound (SMART) goals. SMART goals provide clarity and direction for your work.

4. Time Blocking

Use time blocking to allocate specific time slots to different tasks or projects. This prevents multitasking and enhances focus.

5. Batch Similar Tasks

Group similar tasks together and tackle them in one go. For instance, handle email responses, client meetings, or content creation in dedicated time blocks.

6. Learn to Delegate

Don't be afraid to delegate tasks that others can handle. Virtual assistants or freelance support can free up your time for higher-priority work.

7. Set Deadlines

Establish self-imposed deadlines for tasks to prevent procrastination. Stick to these deadlines as diligently as you would for external ones.

8. Limit Distractions

Identify your primary distractions and take steps to minimize them. This may include turning off notifications, using website blockers, or creating a dedicated workspace.

9. Practice the Two-Minute Rule

If a task takes less than two minutes to complete, do it immediately. This prevents small tasks from piling up and becoming overwhelming.

10. Use Time Management Tools

Explore time management tools and techniques like the Pomodoro method, time tracking apps, or the Getting Things Done (GTD) system to optimize your productivity.

11. Reflect and Adjust

Regularly review your time management strategies and adjust them as needed. What works for you may evolve as you adapt to different destinations and workloads.

Staying Productive on the Road

Productivity is the wind in your sails, propelling you toward your goals as a digital nomad. Here are some tips to help you stay productive while exploring the world:

1. Establish a Morning Routine

Start your day with a morning routine that prepares you for work. This may include exercise, meditation, or a hearty breakfast.

2. Use Task Management Apps

Explore task management apps like Asana, Trello, or Notion to keep track of your projects and deadlines.

3. Create a Weekly Plan

Plan your week in advance, setting specific goals and tasks for each day. This provides a roadmap for your productivity.

4. Embrace Minimalism

Maintain a clutter-free digital workspace. Declutter your desktop, organize your files, and minimize distractions.

5. Set Boundaries with Others

Communicate your work hours and boundaries to friends and fellow travelers. Let them know when you're in the "work zone."

6. Invest in Ergonomics

Invest in ergonomic equipment like an ergonomic chair and a laptop stand to create a comfortable and productive workspace.

7. Focus on Deep Work

Practice deep work, a state of undistracted focus, for tasks that require intense concentration. Dedicate uninterrupted time to these tasks.

8. Manage Energy, Not Just Time

Recognize that your energy levels fluctuate throughout the day. Schedule your most demanding tasks during your peak energy periods.

9. Take Short Walks

Incorporate short walks or breaks into your day. Physical activity can boost creativity and mental clarity.

10. Network and Collaborate

Network with other digital nomads and freelancers. Collaborative work sessions or coworking spaces can provide motivation and accountability.

11. Stay Inspired

Maintain a source of inspiration—a vision board, quotes, or images that remind you of your goals and aspirations.

12. Celebrate Achievements

Celebrate your accomplishments, both big and small. Recognizing your progress can boost your motivation.

13. Learn from Setbacks

View setbacks as opportunities for growth. Learn from mistakes, adapt your strategies, and keep moving forward.

14. Practice Mindfulness

Incorporate mindfulness practices into your day, such as meditation or deep breathing exercises, to reduce stress and enhance focus.

Remember, productivity is not about working harder but working smarter. By setting clear boundaries, managing your time effectively, and adopting productivity-enhancing habits, you'll find the perfect rhythm for balancing work and life on the road.

Chapter 11: Networking and Building Connections

Ahoy, fellow travelers! As a digital nomad, you're on a thrilling journey of self-discovery and exploration, but you don't have to go it alone. In this chapter, we'll dive into the art of networking and building meaningful connections on the road. We'll explore how to find like-minded nomads, make the most of digital nomad meetups and conferences, and build a professional network that spans the globe. So, hoist your social sails, and let's set a course for building connections that enrich your nomadic adventure!

Finding Like-Minded Nomads

One of the joys of the digital nomad lifestyle is the opportunity to connect with people who share your passion for adventure and remote work. Here's how to find like-minded nomads:

1. Join Online Communities

Digital nomad communities on platforms like Facebook, Reddit, and Twitter are treasure troves of fellow nomads. Join these groups to connect with like-minded individuals, ask questions, and share experiences.

2. Attend Co-Living and Co-Working Spaces

Many co-living and co-working spaces cater specifically to digital nomads. Staying in these spaces provides an excellent opportunity to meet fellow travelers and collaborate on projects.

3. Use Networking Apps

Several apps are designed to connect digital nomads in the same location. Apps like NomadList, Meetup, and WiFly Nomads allow you to find and connect with nomads near you.

4. Attend Local Events

Check out local events, workshops, and meetups in your destination. Websites like Eventbrite or local listings can help you discover gatherings where you can meet both locals and fellow nomads.

5. Social Media Hashtags

Search for location-specific hashtags on social media platforms like Instagram and Twitter. You'll find posts from fellow nomads exploring the same area.

6. Leverage Online Platforms

Platforms like LinkedIn and Twitter can be valuable for professional networking. Connect with nomads in your industry or with similar interests.

7. Seek Out Nomad-Friendly Destinations

Some destinations are known hotspots for digital nomads. Places like Bali, Chiang Mai, and Lisbon often have thriving nomad communities.

8. Attend Language or Skill Classes

Taking language or skill classes in your destination can be a great way to meet fellow learners and share experiences.

9. Be Approachable

When you're out and about, whether at a cafe, a beach, or a park, be approachable and strike up conversations with locals and travelers.

10. Nomad Networking Events

Look for networking events specifically designed for digital nomads. These events can provide opportunities to connect both socially and professionally.

Remember, building connections with like-minded nomads can lead to lasting friendships, collaboration on projects, and a support system that makes your nomadic journey even more fulfilling.

Attending Digital Nomad Meetups and Conferences

Digital nomad meetups and conferences are like lighthouses in the sea of nomadic life—they guide you toward valuable connections and knowledge. Here's how to make the most of these gatherings:

1. Research Upcoming Events

Stay updated on upcoming digital nomad meetups and conferences in your current or future destinations. Websites like Meetup, Eventbrite, and Nomad List often list such events.

2. Attend Both Small and Large Gatherings

Smaller meetups offer an intimate setting for networking, while larger conferences can provide access to industry experts and thought leaders.

3. Participate Actively

Don't be a wallflower. Engage actively in conversations, workshops, and panel discussions. Share your insights and ask questions.

4. Bring Business Cards

Yes, they're still relevant! Business cards can make it easy for others to remember you and stay in touch.

5. Volunteer or Speak

Consider volunteering at the event or submitting a proposal to speak if you have expertise to share. Speaking can boost your visibility and credibility.

6. Network Strategically

Set clear networking goals before attending an event. Identify who you'd like to connect with and what you hope to achieve.

7. Join Online Event Groups

Many events have dedicated online groups or forums for attendees. Join these groups in advance to start networking before the event.

8. Follow Up

After the event, follow up with the people you've met. Send personalized messages or connect on LinkedIn to nurture your new connections.

9. Attend Social Events

Many conferences and meetups include social events like dinners, parties, or excursions. Use these opportunities to network in a relaxed setting.

10. Take Notes

During workshops and presentations, take notes on key insights and action items. This not only helps you remember valuable information but also provides conversation starters when networking.

11. Be Open to Learning

Approach these gatherings with a learner's mindset. Attend sessions outside your comfort zone to broaden your knowledge and perspective.

12. Share Your Story

Your journey as a digital nomad is unique. Share your experiences, challenges, and successes with others. Your story can inspire and resonate with fellow nomads.

Building a Professional Network

Your professional network is your compass, guiding you toward opportunities and collaborations. Here's how to build a global professional network:

1. Leverage LinkedIn

Optimize your LinkedIn profile to highlight your skills, experience, and remote work expertise. Connect with professionals you meet along your journey.

2. Attend Industry-Specific Events

Look for conferences or events in your industry or niche. These gatherings can help you connect with professionals who share your interests.

3. Seek Mentorship

Find a mentor in your field or industry who can offer guidance and advice. Mentorship can be invaluable for your professional growth.

4. Collaborate on Projects

Consider collaborating on projects with professionals you meet on your travels. These collaborations can lead to new opportunities and experiences.

5. Attend Workshops and Webinars

Online workshops and webinars are excellent opportunities to expand your knowledge and connect with professionals in your field.

6. Join Online Communities

Participate in online communities related to your industry or interests. Platforms like Reddit, Slack, and specialized forums host industry-specific discussions.

7. Contribute to Blogs or Podcasts

If you're knowledgeable in your field, offer to contribute guest posts to industry blogs or podcasts. This can help you reach a broader audience.

8. Share Your Expertise

Be generous with your knowledge. Share industry insights, tips, and resources with your network. This positions you as a valuable resource.

9. Attend Virtual Conferences

In addition to physical events, explore virtual conferences and summits. They offer opportunities for networking and professional development from anywhere in the world.

10. Create an Online Portfolio

If you're a freelancer or have a creative portfolio, showcase your work online. This provides a convenient way for potential clients or collaborators to see your skills.

11. Be Proactive

Building a professional network requires proactivity. Reach out to professionals you admire, express your interest in their work, and initiate conversations.

12. Follow Up and Stay in Touch

After connecting with professionals, follow up regularly to stay in touch. Send updates on your projects and ask about their endeavors.

Remember, your professional network is a living entity that thrives on genuine connections and mutual support. Whether you're looking for job opportunities, collaborations, or simply a community of like-minded individuals, nurturing your network can open doors you never imagined.

Chapter 12: Health and Wellness on the Road

Ahoy, intrepid travelers! As digital nomads, you're on an epic journey of self-discovery and adventure. But to make the most of your odyssey, you must prioritize something priceless—your health and well-being. In this chapter, we'll embark on a voyage into the realm of maintaining physical and mental health, accessing healthcare while traveling, and staying fit and active on the road. So, grab your compass and let's navigate the seas of well-being together!

Maintaining Physical and Mental Health

Your health is the wind in your sails, propelling you toward your dreams and adventures. Here's how to maintain both your physical and mental well-being:

1. Prioritize Sleep

Quality sleep is the cornerstone of good health. Create a sleep-friendly environment in your accommodation, stick to a regular sleep schedule, and aim for 7-9 hours of sleep per night.

2. Eat Mindfully

Explore local cuisine, but also prioritize nutritious meals. Balance indulgence with wholesome foods to support your energy levels and overall health.

3. Stay Hydrated

Carry a reusable water bottle and drink plenty of water throughout the day. Dehydration can lead to fatigue and decreased cognitive function.

4. Exercise Regularly

Incorporate physical activity into your routine. This can be as simple as daily walks, yoga sessions, or gym workouts. Exercise releases endorphins, boosting your mood and energy levels.

5. Manage Stress

Stress is a natural part of life, but chronic stress can take a toll on your health. Practice stress management techniques like meditation, deep breathing, or mindfulness to stay grounded.

6. Maintain a Work-Life Balance

Set clear boundaries between work and personal time. Avoid overworking, and prioritize leisure activities that bring you joy.

7. Connect with Nature

Spending time in nature can have a rejuvenating effect on your well-being. Seek out green spaces, parks, and beaches during your travels.

8. Seek Social Connections

Maintain meaningful social connections with fellow travelers, locals, and loved ones back home. Loneliness can impact your mental health, so nurture your support system.

9. Practice Mindfulness

Cultivate mindfulness through practices like meditation or journaling. These techniques can help you stay present and reduce anxiety.

10. Monitor Your Mental Health

Pay attention to your mental health. Seek professional help if you experience persistent feelings of sadness, anxiety, or overwhelm.

11. Stay Informed

Research healthcare facilities and emergency services in your destination. Familiarize yourself with local health customs and practices.

12. Carry Necessary Medications

If you have a pre-existing medical condition, ensure you have an adequate supply of medications. Carry a translated prescription if necessary.

13. Purchase Travel Insurance

Invest in comprehensive travel insurance that covers medical emergencies, evacuation, and unexpected cancellations. Read the policy carefully to understand the coverage.

14. Locate Local Hospitals and Clinics

Know the location of local hospitals, clinics, and pharmacies in your area. Keep their contact information readily available.

15. Learn Basic Medical Phrases

If you're traveling to a non-English-speaking country, learn basic medical phrases in the local language. This can be invaluable in emergencies.

16. Stay Vaccinated

Stay up-to-date on vaccinations recommended for your travel destinations. Some countries may require specific vaccinations for entry.

17. Practice Safe Food and Water Hygiene

To avoid foodborne illnesses, practice safe food and water hygiene. Wash your hands regularly, eat at reputable establishments, and drink bottled or purified water if necessary.

18. Be Cautious with Activities

Participate in adventure activities and sports cautiously. Ensure you receive proper safety equipment and guidance from reputable providers.

19. Protect Your Skin

Apply sunscreen, wear protective clothing, and stay hydrated to protect your skin from the sun's harmful effects.

20. Stay Informed About Local Health Risks

Keep abreast of local health advisories, such as disease outbreaks or environmental hazards, and take necessary precautions.

21. Carry a First Aid Kit

Pack a basic first aid kit with essentials like bandages, antiseptic wipes, pain relievers, and any personal medications.

Staying Fit and Active

Staying active on the road can be a delightful adventure in itself. Here's how to keep your body moving and maintain your fitness:

1. Explore on Foot or by Bike

Walking or cycling is an excellent way to explore your destination while staying active. Opt for self-guided tours on foot or rent a bike to discover the local sights.

2. Try Local Activities

Embrace local activities like hiking, swimming, or practicing martial arts. These experiences not only keep you fit but also immerse you in the culture.

3. Use Fitness Apps

Download fitness apps that offer guided workouts you can do anywhere. Apps like Nike Training Club or Fitbod provide a variety of exercise routines.

4. Find a Local Gym or Studio

Many destinations have gyms or fitness studios where you can purchase day passes or short-term memberships. Use these facilities to maintain your workout routine.

5. Practice Yoga or Pilates

Yoga and Pilates require minimal equipment and can be practiced in your accommodation or in outdoor spaces. These disciplines improve flexibility, strength, and mindfulness.

6. Swim in Natural Waters

Seek out natural bodies of water like lakes, rivers, or oceans for swimming. Swimming is a full-body workout that's gentle on the joints.

7. Dance Your Heart Out

Attend dance classes or find local dance clubs to dance the night away. Dancing is a fun way to stay active and connect with locals.

8. Carry Resistance Bands

Compact resistance bands are lightweight and versatile for strength training. They take up little space in your luggage and can be used for a full-body workout.

9. Participate in Local Races

Check if there are any local running races, marathons, or fun runs happening during your stay. Participating can be a memorable fitness challenge.

10. Incorporate Bodyweight Exercises

Bodyweight exercises like push-ups, squats, and planks require no equipment and can be done in your accommodation or outdoor spaces.

11. Embrace Adventure Sports

If you're an adrenaline junkie, try adventure sports like rock climbing, surfing, or zip-lining. These activities offer a thrilling workout.

12. Stay Consistent

Create a fitness routine that suits your travel schedule. Consistency is key, so aim to work out a few times a week to maintain your fitness level.

13. Stay Hydrated and Eat Well

Nourish your body with balanced meals and stay hydrated to support your fitness goals. Fueling your body properly is essential for performance.

14. Listen to Your Body

Pay attention to your body's signals. If you're tired or sore, give yourself permission to rest and recover.

15. Enjoy Active Travel

Plan travel activities that involve physical exertion, like hiking to a scenic viewpoint or exploring ancient ruins on foot.

Remember, your health is your most valuable asset, and nurturing it allows you to make the most of your nomadic journey. By prioritizing physical and mental well-being, staying prepared for healthcare needs, and staying active on the road, you'll not only enjoy your adventures to the fullest but also create a strong foundation for a fulfilling digital nomad lifestyle.

Chapter 13: Exploring New Cultures

Ahoy, culture connoisseurs! As digital nomads, your journey isn't just about working remotely; it's also an exhilarating expedition into the rich tapestry of global cultures. In this chapter, we'll delve into the art of exploring new cultures, embracing cultural experiences, learning languages and local customs, and practicing responsible tourism and cultural sensitivity. So, don your cultural explorer hat, and let's set sail into the vibrant world of cross-cultural encounters!

Embracing Cultural Experiences

One of the most rewarding aspects of the digital nomad lifestyle is the opportunity to immerse yourself in diverse cultures. Here's how to embrace and savor these experiences:

1. Be Curious and Open-Minded

Approach each new culture with curiosity and an open heart. Be willing to learn, adapt, and embrace different ways of life.

2. Engage with Locals

Strike up conversations with locals and fellow travelers. Ask questions, listen to their stories, and seek to understand their perspectives.

3. Try Local Cuisine

Food is a gateway to culture. Savor local dishes, street food, and delicacies to experience the flavors of your destination.

4. Attend Cultural Events

Keep an eye out for cultural festivals, art exhibitions, and performances happening in your destination. Participate to get a taste of local traditions.

5. Learn Traditional Crafts

Consider taking workshops to learn traditional crafts or skills like cooking, pottery, or dance. It's a hands-on way to connect with a culture's heritage.

6. Explore Historical Sites

Visit historical sites, museums, and landmarks to gain insights into a culture's past and its impact on the present.

7. Participate in Local Rituals

If appropriate, join in local rituals or ceremonies. This can provide a profound glimpse into the spiritual and cultural aspects of a community.

8. Travel Slowly

Avoid rushing from one tourist attraction to another. Travel slowly to give yourself time to absorb the local atmosphere and way of life.

9. Stay with Locals

Consider staying with local hosts through platforms like Airbnb or homestays. This offers a more authentic and immersive experience.

10. Read About the Culture

Read books, articles, or blogs about the culture of your destination before and during your stay. This background knowledge can enhance your appreciation.

11. Take Cultural Tours

Join guided cultural tours led by knowledgeable locals. These tours often provide insights that you might miss on your own.

12. Volunteer Locally

Volunteering with local organizations can deepen your connection with the community and allow you to give back.

13. Document Your Experiences

Keep a journal, take photos, or create a travel blog to document your cultural discoveries. Sharing your experiences can inspire others and help you remember your journey.

14. Be Respectful

Respect local customs, traditions, and etiquettes, even if they differ from your own. Show appreciation for the culture you're visiting.

Learning Languages and Local Customs

Learning the language and customs of your host country is like opening a door to deeper cultural understanding. Here's how to go about it:

1. Learn Basic Phrases

Start with basic greetings, polite expressions, and common phrases in the local language. Locals appreciate the effort, even if you make mistakes.

2. Take Language Classes

Enroll in language classes or find language exchange partners to improve your language skills. Learning the local language can greatly enrich your experience.

3. Use Language Apps

Language learning apps like Duolingo, Rosetta Stone, or Babbel can be convenient tools for studying on the go.

4. Practice with Locals

Engage in conversations with locals to practice your language skills. Don't be afraid to make mistakes; it's all part of the learning process.

5. Immerse Yourself

Surround yourself with the language as much as possible. Change your phone's language settings, watch local TV shows, and read newspapers or books in the local language.

6. Study Local Customs

Take the time to understand local customs, etiquettes, and taboos. Being culturally aware helps you navigate social situations with respect.

7. Observe and Learn

Observe how locals interact, greet each other, and handle various situations. Learning by observation can be just as valuable as formal education.

8. Ask for Guidance

If you're unsure about local customs, don't hesitate to ask locals or expats for guidance. Most people are happy to help you understand their culture.

9. Adapt to Dress Codes

Respect dress codes, especially in religious or conservative areas. Dress modestly when required, and adhere to local norms.

10. Show Appreciation

Express your appreciation for the local culture. Participate in traditions, share your own cultural experiences, and foster cross-cultural exchange.

Responsible Tourism and Cultural Sensitivity

With great cultural exploration comes great responsibility. Here's how to practice responsible tourism and cultural sensitivity:

1. Research Your Destination

Before traveling, research the history, culture, and social issues of your destination. Understanding the context can inform responsible behavior.

2. Respect Local Laws

Obey local laws and regulations, even if they differ from your own country's. Ignorance of the law is not an excuse.

3. Support Local Businesses

Opt to support local businesses, artisans, and vendors. This contributes to the local economy and helps preserve cultural traditions.

4. Be Mindful of Photography

Always ask for permission before taking photos of people, especially in sensitive or private situations. Respect their privacy.

5. Leave No Trace

Practice Leave No Trace principles when exploring natural areas. Minimize your impact on the environment and local wildlife.

6. Avoid Cultural Appropriation

Be aware of cultural appropriation, which involves borrowing elements of one culture without understanding or respecting their significance.

7. Avoid Exploitative Tourism

Steer clear of exploitative tourist activities that harm animals, the environment, or local communities.

8. Give Back Ethically

If you wish to volunteer or give back to the community, choose ethical and reputable organizations that prioritize local empowerment and sustainability.

9. Engage in Meaningful Interactions

Instead of just passing through, seek meaningful interactions with locals. Engage in conversations and learn from each other.

10. Show Humility and Respect

Approach cultural exchanges with humility and respect. Remember that you're a guest in someone else's home.

11. Educate Others

Share your knowledge and experiences of responsible tourism and cultural sensitivity with fellow travelers. Encourage responsible behavior in your community.

12. Be an Ambassador

As a digital nomad, you're an ambassador of your home country. Showcase the best qualities of your culture and foster goodwill.

Cultural exploration is a thrilling part of the digital nomad lifestyle. By embracing cultural experiences, learning languages and local customs, and practicing responsible tourism and cultural sensitivity, you not only enrich your own journey but also contribute positively to the communities you visit. So, continue your cultural voyage with an open heart and a thirst for understanding.

Chapter 14: Long-Term Planning

Ahoy, wise wanderers! While the digital nomadic lifestyle is a thrilling adventure, it's essential to set your sights on the horizon and plan for the long term. In this chapter, we'll explore the crucial aspects of long-term planning for digital nomads. We'll dive into retirement and future financial security, discuss the art of transitioning out of digital nomadism, and guide you on creating a sustainable lifestyle that allows you to continue thriving, wherever your journey takes you.

Retirement and Future Financial Security

Retirement might seem like a distant speck on your nomadic horizon, but it's a destination worth planning for. Here's how to navigate the waters of financial security:

1. Set Retirement Goals

Begin by defining your retirement goals. How do you envision your life in retirement? What activities do you want to pursue, and where would you like to live?

2. Create a Retirement Savings Plan

Consider opening a dedicated retirement account, such as an IRA or a self-employed 401(k). Contribute regularly to build a nest egg for your future.

3. Diversify Your Investments

Diversification can help mitigate risks in your investment portfolio. Explore a mix of stocks, bonds, real estate, and other assets.

4. Seek Professional Advice

Consult a financial advisor who specializes in working with digital nomads. They can help you create a personalized retirement plan.

5. Plan for Healthcare

Research healthcare options for retirees, especially if you plan to retire in a different country. Understand how your healthcare needs will be met.

6. Consider Income Streams

Explore opportunities to create passive income streams that can support your retirement. This could include investments, royalties, or online businesses.

7. Budget for Longevity

Plan for a longer life expectancy by ensuring your savings will last throughout retirement. Adjust your budget and investment strategies accordingly.

8. Stay Informed

Stay updated on changes in tax laws, investment trends, and retirement planning strategies. Being informed can help you make informed decisions.

9. Prepare for Emergencies

Have an emergency fund in place to cover unexpected expenses in retirement. Aim for at least three to six months' worth of living expenses.

10. Stay Debt-Free

Work towards being debt-free by the time you retire. Pay off high-interest debts, such as credit cards, to reduce financial stress in retirement.

11. Reevaluate Regularly

Periodically review your retirement plan and make adjustments as needed. Your goals and financial situation may change over time.

12. Consider Downsizing

As you approach retirement, consider downsizing your living arrangements to reduce expenses and free up equity.

13. Create an Estate Plan

Prepare a will, designate beneficiaries, and plan for the distribution of your assets in the event of your passing.

14. Plan for Social Security

Understand how Social Security benefits work for digital nomads and factor them into your retirement income planning.

15. Build a Support System

Connect with other digital nomads who are planning for retirement. Sharing insights and experiences can be valuable.

Transitioning Out of Digital Nomadism

As your journey evolves, you might find yourself considering the transition out of digital nomadism. Here's how to navigate this phase:

1. Reflect on Your Goals

Take time to reflect on your long-term goals, both personally and professionally. What do you want to achieve in this new phase of life?

2. Consider a Home Base

If you plan to settle in one location, consider establishing a home base where you can build a sense of community and stability.

3. Maintain Flexibility

While transitioning, maintain flexibility in your plans. You can continue to travel part-time or take extended trips while maintaining a base.

4. Plan for Career Changes

Explore career opportunities or businesses that align with your new goals. Consider how your skills and experiences as a nomad can benefit your future endeavors.

5. Evaluate Your Finances

Review your financial situation and make adjustments based on your transition plans. Ensure you have the resources you need for this new phase.

6. Build a Support Network

Connect with others who have transitioned from the digital nomad lifestyle. They can offer guidance and insights into the process.

7. Focus on Health and Wellness

Prioritize your health and well-being as you transition. Establish routines that support your physical and mental health.

8. Embrace Change

Embrace the changes that come with transitioning. Recognize that it's a natural evolution of your journey.

9. Seek Professional Guidance

If needed, consult with career counselors or life coaches who specialize in transitions. They can help you navigate this phase effectively.

10. Stay True to Your Values

Ensure that your transition aligns with your values and aspirations. This will help you create a fulfilling and meaningful next chapter.

Creating a Sustainable Lifestyle

As a digital nomad, sustainability is not just about protecting the environment—it's also about maintaining a lifestyle that supports your well-being. Here's how to create a sustainable nomadic life:

1. Adopt Minimalism

Embrace minimalism by decluttering your possessions and simplifying your life. Travel light and focus on experiences over material possessions.

2. Reduce Your Environmental Footprint

Practice eco-friendly habits like reducing plastic use, conserving energy and water, and supporting sustainable tourism.

3. Support Local Economies

Prioritize spending on local businesses and artisans, which contributes to the economic sustainability of the communities you visit.

4. Embrace Slow Travel

Opt for longer stays in each destination rather than constantly moving. Slow travel allows for deeper cultural immersion and reduces your carbon footprint.

5. Plan Thoughtfully

Plan your travel routes and accommodations thoughtfully to minimize unnecessary travel-related emissions.

6. Volunteer or Give Back

Give back to the communities you visit through volunteering or supporting local initiatives. Leave a positive impact on the places you explore.

7. Practice Work-Life Balance

Maintain a healthy work-life balance to prevent burnout. Balance work commitments with leisure and exploration.

8. Stay Physically Active

Incorporate physical activity into your daily routine, whether it's yoga, hiking, or other forms of exercise. A healthy body supports a sustainable lifestyle.

9. Nurture Relationships

Prioritize relationships with loved ones, whether they're traveling with you or back home. Strong connections contribute to your emotional sustainability.

10. Focus on Personal Growth

Continue to invest in your personal growth and development. Learning new skills and perspectives enhances your nomadic journey.

11. Adapt to Change

Stay adaptable and open to change. The ability to adjust to new environments and circumstances is a hallmark of sustainability.

12. Reflect and Evolve

Regularly reflect on your nomadic lifestyle and make adjustments as needed to ensure it aligns with your evolving values and goals.

Long-term planning for digital nomads isn't just about preparing for retirement; it's about crafting a life that encompasses financial security, purposeful transitions, and sustainability. By setting clear retirement goals, navigating the transition process with intention, and creating a sustainable nomadic lifestyle, you'll be well-equipped to navigate the ever-changing seas of the digital nomad journey.

As you continue to explore new horizons and embrace the transformative power of this lifestyle, remember that every step you take is a part of your unique journey. So, chart your course with wisdom and intention, and let your nomadic adventure unfold with purpose and fulfillment.

Chapter 15: Environmental Responsibility

As digital nomads, our journeys are fueled by wanderlust, but it's our responsibility to ensure our adventures don't harm the very planet we explore. In this chapter, we'll delve into the critical topic of environmental responsibility for digital nomads. We'll explore ways to reduce your carbon footprint while roaming the globe, adopt sustainable travel practices, and support eco-friendly initiatives that preserve the natural beauty of our planet.

Reducing Your Carbon Footprint as a Nomad

Digital nomads are known for their freedom to roam, but it's essential to roam responsibly. Here's how to minimize your carbon footprint while living the nomadic lifestyle:

1. Choose Sustainable Transportation

Opt for eco-friendly transportation options whenever possible. Consider trains, buses, or carpooling instead of domestic flights. If you must fly, book direct flights to reduce emissions.

2. Travel Slowly

Slow travel not only allows for a deeper connection with local cultures but also reduces your carbon footprint. Spend more time in each destination to cut down on frequent travel.

3. Embrace Alternative Modes of Transport

Explore destinations on foot, by bicycle, or through public transportation. It's a fantastic way to minimize emissions and engage with the local community.

4. Offset Your Carbon Emissions

Support carbon offset programs that invest in renewable energy, reforestation, or other sustainability initiatives. Calculate your carbon emissions and contribute accordingly.

5. Pack Light

Traveling with less luggage reduces fuel consumption, especially when flying. Opt for versatile clothing and pack only what you truly need.

6. Choose Eco-Friendly Accommodations

Stay in eco-friendly accommodations that implement sustainable practices, such as energy-efficient lighting, water conservation, and waste reduction.

7. Conserve Water and Energy

Be mindful of water and energy use in accommodations. Take shorter showers, turn off lights when not in use, and reduce air conditioning or heating.

8. Reduce Plastic Use

Carry a reusable water bottle, shopping bag, and utensils to minimize single-use plastic waste. Avoid products with excessive packaging.

9. Support Sustainable Tour Operators

Choose tour operators and activities that prioritize environmental conservation and responsible tourism practices.

10. Reduce Food Waste

Order meals mindfully and avoid food waste. Share dishes if portions are large, and carry reusable containers for leftovers.

11. Participate in Clean-Up Efforts

Join local clean-up initiatives to give back to the places you visit. Participating in beach clean-ups or environmental projects is a meaningful way to contribute.

12. Use Eco-Friendly Toiletries

Pack eco-friendly toiletries like biodegradable soaps and shampoos. These products have a smaller environmental impact.

13. Dispose of Waste Responsibly

Follow proper waste disposal practices in every destination. Research local recycling and waste management guidelines.

14. Educate Yourself

Stay informed about environmental issues and conservation efforts in the regions you visit. Knowledge empowers you to make responsible choices.

15. Be an Advocate

Share your commitment to environmental responsibility with fellow travelers and encourage them to join your efforts.

Sustainable Travel Practices

Sustainable travel is about enjoying the world while leaving it better than you found it. Here's how to incorporate sustainable practices into your nomadic lifestyle:

1. Support Eco-Friendly Destinations

Choose destinations that prioritize sustainability and environmental protection. Research places that have received eco-certifications.

2. Shop Locally

Support local artisans, markets, and businesses. Purchasing locally-made products and souvenirs contributes to the local economy.

3. Respect Wildlife

Observe wildlife from a safe distance and never engage in activities that harm animals or their habitats. Avoid activities involving captive or exploited animals.

4. Leave No Trace

Practice the Leave No Trace principles, which include packing out what you pack in, staying on designated trails, and avoiding damage to natural areas.

5. Conserve Energy

Turn off lights and appliances when not in use, and minimize air conditioning or heating in accommodations.

6. Respect Cultural Heritage

Admire and learn from cultural heritage sites without damaging or removing artifacts. Observe local customs and etiquette.

7. Choose Sustainable Food Options

Dine at restaurants that prioritize locally-sourced, sustainable, and organic foods. Support establishments that reduce food waste.

8. Stay in Green Accommodations

Select accommodations that have eco-friendly practices, such as using renewable energy, conserving water, and recycling.

9. Use Public Transportation

Opt for public transportation or eco-friendly options like electric scooters or bicycles for exploring urban areas.

10. Practice Responsible Diving and Snorkeling

If you're into water sports, choose operators that adhere to responsible diving and snorkeling practices. Avoid touching or damaging coral reefs.

11. Volunteer for Conservation

Consider volunteering with conservation organizations during your travels. Help protect natural habitats and wildlife.

12. Advocate for Sustainable Travel

Support and engage with organizations that promote sustainable travel practices. Advocate for responsible tourism within the digital nomad community.

Supporting Eco-Friendly Initiatives

As digital nomads, we can make a positive impact by supporting eco-friendly initiatives around the world. Here's how to get involved:

1. Join Environmental Organizations

Become a member of or contribute to environmental organizations dedicated to conservation, climate action, and sustainability.

2. Participate in Reforestation

Support reforestation efforts by donating to tree-planting initiatives. Trees are essential for carbon sequestration and biodiversity.

3. Volunteer for Conservation

Participate in conservation projects during your travels. Volunteer opportunities abound, from wildlife sanctuaries to beach clean-ups.

4. Support Sustainable Tourism

Choose to support businesses and destinations that prioritize sustainable tourism. Share your experiences and encourage others to do the same.

5. Donate to Green Causes

Allocate a portion of your income or savings to environmental causes you believe in. Your contributions can make a significant difference.

6. Reduce Your Digital Carbon Footprint

Digital nomads often rely heavily on technology. Minimize your digital carbon footprint by using energy-efficient devices and servers.

7. Advocate for Change

Advocate for eco-friendly practices within the digital nomad community. Encourage others to adopt responsible travel habits.

8. Educate and Inspire

Share your knowledge and passion for environmental responsibility with fellow nomads and travelers. Inspire others to make a positive impact.

9. Support Sustainable Products

Choose eco-friendly products and brands that prioritize sustainability, whether it's clothing, electronics, or everyday items.

10. Offset Your Travel

Calculate the carbon emissions from your travels and offset them by contributing to carbon offset projects.

Remember, every small action counts when it comes to environmental responsibility. By reducing your carbon footprint, adopting sustainable travel practices, and supporting eco-friendly initiatives, you can help preserve the breathtaking landscapes and diverse ecosystems that make our planet so extraordinary.

As digital nomads, we have the unique opportunity to not only explore the world but also protect it for future generations of travelers. So, set sail with a commitment to environmental responsibility, and let your journey leave a positive mark on the planet we all call home.

Chapter 16: Success Stories and Case Studies

Ahoy, fellow nomads! As we sail through the digital nomad seas, it's always inspiring to look to those who have gone before us and made their own mark on this adventurous lifestyle. In this chapter, we'll delve into the captivating world of success stories and case studies of digital nomads. These tales of triumph will not only fuel your wanderlust but also provide valuable insights into how real-life nomads have achieved location-independent success.

Inspiring Stories of Successful Digital Nomads

Let's embark on a journey through the stories of remarkable individuals who have turned their nomadic dreams into reality. These success stories serve as beacons of inspiration for all aspiring digital nomads.

Story 1: The Freelance Maverick - Sarah's Odyssey

Sarah had always been a creative soul. She started her journey as a freelance writer, crafting articles and blog posts for various clients while working a traditional office job. However, her passion for writing and her thirst for adventure led her to take the plunge into the digital nomad lifestyle.

With her laptop as her trusty companion, Sarah set off on her nomadic adventure, exploring exotic destinations while continuing her freelance work. As she traveled, she expanded her skill set by learning about SEO and digital marketing. Over time, she began to take on more substantial projects and higher-paying clients.

Today, Sarah has built a thriving freelance career that allows her to work from anywhere in the world. She's not only financially secure but

97

also living her dream of exploring new cultures and landscapes. Her story serves as a testament to the power of determination and passion.

Story 2: The Tech Trailblazer - Alex's Journey

Alex had always been fascinated by technology and coding. He started his career as a software developer at a tech company but soon realized that he wanted more flexibility in his work and life. That's when he decided to become a digital nomad.

Alex honed his coding skills and began freelancing as a web developer. His expertise in web development quickly gained recognition, and he started landing high-paying remote contracts. This newfound freedom allowed him to travel extensively, from bustling cities to serene beach towns.

Eventually, Alex leveraged his experience to launch his own tech startup. With a team of remote developers and designers from around the world, he created a successful product that revolutionized the industry. Alex's story demonstrates that the digital nomad lifestyle can be a launchpad for entrepreneurial success.

Story 3: The Globetrotting Educator - Emma's Expedition

Emma was a passionate educator who yearned to make a global impact. She started her journey by teaching English as a foreign language online while living in her home country. However, she craved the excitement of exploring new cultures firsthand.

Emma transitioned into becoming a digital nomad by teaching English remotely while traveling. She carefully planned her lessons to accommodate different time zones and kept a flexible schedule to accommodate her nomadic lifestyle.

Over time, Emma's reputation as a skilled educator grew, and she started offering online courses and workshops. Her audience expanded beyond borders, attracting students from around the world. Emma's story is a testament to how the digital nomad lifestyle can empower educators to reach a global audience and make a lasting impact.

Learning from Their Journeys

These success stories offer valuable lessons and insights for aspiring digital nomads:

1. Passion and Persistence

Passion is the driving force behind success. All three nomads followed their passions and didn't give up when faced with challenges.

2. Skill Development

Continuously improving your skills is crucial. Sarah, Alex, and Emma expanded their skill sets to become more valuable in their respective fields.

3. Remote Work Opportunities

Remote work can be the gateway to a nomadic lifestyle. Starting with remote jobs or freelance work can provide the financial stability needed for travel.

4. Entrepreneurship

Consider entrepreneurial opportunities. Alex's startup journey highlights how a nomadic lifestyle can be a fertile ground for launching a successful business.

5. Online Education

The digital nomad lifestyle isn't limited to tech or creative fields. Emma's story shows that educators can have a global impact by embracing online education.

6. Adaptability and Flexibility

Being adaptable and flexible is essential. Digital nomads must adapt to different time zones, work environments, and challenges while maintaining a positive attitude.

7. Networking and Collaboration

Building a network and collaborating with professionals in your field can open doors to exciting opportunities. Networking played a significant role in the success of these nomads.

8. Time Management

Effective time management is key. Nomads often juggle work, travel, and personal exploration, so mastering time management is crucial.

Real-Life Examples of Location-Independent Careers

Let's explore a few more real-life case studies of location-independent careers to showcase the diverse possibilities available to digital nomads:

Case Study 1: The Virtual Assistant - Maria's Journey

Maria, a virtual assistant, provides administrative support to small businesses and entrepreneurs. Her tasks include managing emails, scheduling appointments, and handling social media accounts. Maria enjoys the flexibility of her work, which allows her to travel and work from various locations.

Case Study 2: The Graphic Designer - Carlos's Expedition

Carlos is a graphic designer who creates visual content for clients worldwide. His design projects range from branding and marketing materials to website graphics. By freelancing as a graphic designer, Carlos can take his work on the road and explore new destinations while delivering top-notch designs.

Case Study 3: The Travel Blogger - Lisa's Odyssey

Lisa is a travel blogger and influencer who documents her adventures on her blog and social media platforms. She collaborates with travel brands and tourism boards to promote destinations. Her nomadic lifestyle allows her to authentically share her travel experiences with her audience while earning an income from sponsored content and affiliate marketing.

Case Study 4: The E-commerce Entrepreneur - Raj's Journey

Raj runs an e-commerce business that sells handmade artisanal goods. He sources products from artisans in different countries and sells them through his online store. Raj manages his business remotely and travels to meet artisans, attend trade fairs, and explore potential markets.

Case Study 5: The Online Consultant - Elena's Expedition

Elena offers online consulting services in the field of sustainable agriculture. She advises farmers and agricultural organizations on eco-friendly practices. Her expertise allows her to work remotely while assisting clients around the world in improving their agricultural practices.

These case studies demonstrate the diverse range of careers and professions that can be pursued as a digital nomad. The key to success lies in finding a location-independent career that aligns with your skills, passions, and lifestyle goals.

As you chart your own course as a digital nomad, remember that these success stories and case studies are not just tales of achievement but also blueprints for your own journey.

Chapter 17: Legal and Regulatory Considerations

Ahoy, intrepid travelers! While the digital nomadic lifestyle offers unparalleled freedom and adventure, it's essential to sail these nomadic seas with a clear understanding of the legal and regulatory waters. In this chapter, we'll dive into the critical topic of legal and regulatory considerations for digital nomads. We'll explore how to navigate legal issues, address tax implications and legal structures, and ensure compliance with local regulations while you explore the world.

Navigating Legal Issues as a Digital Nomad

As a digital nomad, you'll encounter various legal issues and challenges. Here's how to chart your course through these waters:

1. Visa and Immigration

Understanding visa and immigration requirements is crucial. Research the visa policies of the countries you plan to visit. Some countries offer specific visas for digital nomads, while others may require business or tourist visas. Ensure you comply with visa regulations and extend your visa if needed.

2. Remote Work Legality

Research the legal status of remote work in your home country and the countries you visit. Some countries have specific regulations regarding remote work and income earned abroad. Comply with tax and labor laws to avoid legal issues.

3. Business Registration

If you operate a business as a digital nomad, consider registering it in a tax-efficient jurisdiction. Consult with legal and financial experts to determine the best structure for your business, such as a sole proprietorship, LLC, or corporation.

4. Contracts and Agreements

When freelancing or providing services, use clear and legally binding contracts. Contracts protect both you and your clients by outlining expectations, deliverables, payment terms, and dispute resolution procedures.

5. Intellectual Property

Protect your intellectual property, such as written content, designs, or inventions, by understanding copyright, trademark, and patent laws in different countries. Register your intellectual property when necessary.

6. Taxes

Tax regulations can be complex for digital nomads. Consult with a tax professional who specializes in international tax law to ensure compliance. Be aware of tax treaties between your home country and the countries you visit to prevent double taxation.

7. Banking and Financial Transactions

Maintain separate bank accounts for personal and business finances. Use online banking services and notify your bank of your travel plans to avoid account freezes due to suspicious international transactions.

8. Health and Travel Insurance

Ensure you have adequate health insurance that covers you while traveling. Review the terms and conditions of your insurance policy to understand coverage limitations and exclusions.

9. Privacy and Data Security

Protect your digital identity and data while traveling. Use secure Wi-Fi networks, enable two-factor authentication, and encrypt sensitive information. Be aware of data protection laws in different countries.

10. Contracts with Accommodations

Read and understand the terms and conditions of your accommodation bookings. Some countries have specific regulations governing short-term rentals, so ensure your bookings comply with local laws.

11. Environmental Regulations

Respect environmental regulations, such as restrictions on wildlife interactions or protected natural areas. Engaging in activities that harm the environment can lead to legal consequences.

12. Legal Representation

In case of legal issues, consider having access to legal representation in both your home country and the countries you visit. Legal issues may arise in various contexts, from business disputes to immigration matters.

Navigating legal issues as a digital nomad requires diligence and awareness. While the nomadic lifestyle offers incredible freedom, it also comes with responsibilities to adhere to the laws and regulations of the countries you visit.

Tax Implications and Legal Structures

Understanding the tax implications of the digital nomad lifestyle is essential to avoid unexpected financial setbacks. Here's how to navigate tax considerations and choose the right legal structures:

1. Tax Residency

Determine your tax residency status in your home country. Some countries have specific rules for individuals who are no longer considered tax residents.

2. Double Taxation

Research tax treaties between your home country and the countries you visit. These treaties can help prevent double taxation on income earned abroad.

3. Tax Planning

Consult with a tax advisor or accountant experienced in international taxation. They can help you create a tax-efficient plan and structure your finances to minimize tax liabilities legally.

4. Legal Business Structures

If you operate a business, choose a legal structure that aligns with your tax and liability preferences. Options include sole proprietorships, partnerships, LLCs, corporations, and more.

5. Nomad-Friendly Countries

Consider basing your business in a country with favorable tax laws for digital nomads, such as those that offer low or no corporate income tax.

6. Record Keeping

Maintain accurate records of your income, expenses, and tax payments. Proper record-keeping is crucial for tax compliance and can help in case of audits.

7. Tax Filing Deadlines

Stay informed about tax filing deadlines in both your home country and the countries you visit. Missing deadlines can lead to penalties and legal issues.

8. VAT/GST

Understand value-added tax (VAT) or goods and services tax (GST) regulations in the countries you visit, especially if you sell products or services internationally.

9. Digital Nomad Tax Services

Consider using specialized tax services designed for digital nomads. These services can simplify tax compliance and provide guidance on tax optimization.

10. Legal Compliance

Ensure your business and financial activities comply with the laws and regulations of the countries you visit. Seek legal counsel if you have specific concerns.

11. Bank Accounts

Open bank accounts in countries with favorable banking regulations for international transactions and currency exchange.

Navigating tax implications and legal structures can be complex, but with proper planning and professional guidance, you can manage your financial affairs efficiently while enjoying the benefits of the digital nomad lifestyle.

Compliance with Local Regulations

Compliance with local regulations is essential to maintain a harmonious and lawful presence in the countries you visit. Here are key areas of compliance to consider:

1. Visa and Immigration Compliance

Follow the visa and immigration regulations of the countries you visit. Overstaying a visa or working without the proper permits can lead to deportation or fines.

2. Local Tax Compliance

If you earn income in a foreign country, comply with local tax laws and reporting requirements. Failure to do so may result in legal penalties.

3. Business Licensing

If you operate a business in a foreign country, research and obtain the necessary business licenses and permits. Compliance with local business regulations is essential.

4. Local Employment Laws

If you hire local employees or freelancers, adhere to local labor laws, including wage and hour regulations, working conditions, and benefits.

5. Cultural and Social Norms

Respect local customs and cultural norms. Familiarize yourself with acceptable behavior, dress codes, and etiquette in each country you visit.

6. Environmental Regulations

Follow environmental regulations in each destination. Respect protected areas, wildlife, and natural resources.

7. Health and Safety Regulations

Adhere to health and safety regulations, especially if you engage in activities like scuba diving or adventure sports. Ensure you have proper insurance coverage for these activities.

8. Internet and Digital Laws

Be aware of internet and digital laws in each country. Some countries may have restrictions on content, online activities, or social media usage.

9. Accommodation Regulations

Observe regulations related to accommodations, including check-in/check-out times, visitor policies, and property use.

10. Social Responsibility

Engage in responsible tourism and support local communities. Contribute positively to the destinations you visit by respecting local traditions and minimizing your environmental impact.

11. Local Authorities

Cooperate with local authorities and law enforcement if you encounter legal issues or emergencies. Maintaining a respectful and cooperative attitude can be beneficial.

Navigating legal and regulatory considerations as a digital nomad requires vigilance, research, and a willingness to adapt to different legal systems and cultural norms. Staying informed and seeking professional guidance when needed will help you navigate these waters smoothly.

As you embark on your journey as a digital nomad, remember that understanding and respecting the legal and regulatory landscape is a crucial part of preserving the freedom and opportunities that come with location independence.

Chapter 18: Evolving Technologies and Trends

Ahoy, tech-savvy nomads! In the ever-changing landscape of digital nomadism, staying ahead of the curve is crucial. In this chapter, we'll dive into the exciting world of evolving technologies and trends that are shaping the digital nomad lifestyle. We'll explore the latest tools and platforms, the profound impact of remote work trends, and how to prepare for future changes as you continue your nomadic journey.

Emerging Tools and Platforms for Digital Nomads

As a digital nomad, your toolkit is your treasure chest, and it's constantly evolving. Let's open that chest and discover some of the emerging tools and platforms that can enhance your nomadic experience:

1. Remote Work Platforms

The rise of remote work has led to the emergence of platforms like Slack, Microsoft Teams, and Zoom. These tools facilitate seamless communication, collaboration, and virtual meetings with colleagues and clients worldwide.

2. Co-Working Spaces

Co-working spaces are no longer a novelty; they're a necessity for digital nomads. Platforms like WeWork and local co-working hubs offer flexible, professional workspaces with high-speed internet and networking opportunities.

3. Digital Nomad Communities

Online communities and forums dedicated to digital nomads provide a space for networking, sharing tips, and seeking advice. Platforms like Reddit's r/digitalnomad and Nomad List are valuable resources.

4. Travel Apps and Services

Apps like Airbnb, Booking.com, and Skyscanner help digital nomads find accommodation, flights, and transportation options conveniently. Travel insurance apps and services are also essential for peace of mind on the road.

5. Digital Wallets and Cryptocurrency

Digital nomads often deal with international currencies. Digital wallets like PayPal and cryptocurrencies like Bitcoin offer secure and convenient ways to manage finances and make international transactions.

6. Language Learning Apps

Learning the local language enhances your cultural experience and facilitates communication. Duolingo, Babbel, and Rosetta Stone are popular language learning apps.

7. Project Management Tools

Tools like Trello, Asana, and Monday.com assist in project management, task organization, and team collaboration, enabling efficient remote work.

8. Time Zone Converters

Navigating different time zones can be challenging. Time zone converter apps simplify scheduling by displaying multiple time zones simultaneously.

9. Mobile Hotspots

A reliable mobile hotspot or pocket Wi-Fi device ensures you stay connected even in remote areas with limited internet access.

10. Online Learning Platforms

Platforms like Coursera, Udemy, and edX offer opportunities for skill development and professional growth while on the road.

11. VPN Services

Virtual private networks (VPNs) enhance online security and privacy, crucial for nomads who frequently connect to public Wi-Fi networks.

12. E-commerce Platforms

For digital nomads running online businesses, e-commerce platforms like Shopify and WooCommerce simplify product sales and management.

13. Social Media Tools

Social media scheduling tools like Buffer and Hootsuite help you maintain a consistent online presence while managing multiple accounts.

14. Travel Blogs and Vlogs

Blogging platforms like WordPress and vlogging platforms like YouTube offer creative outlets for sharing your nomadic experiences and generating income.

15. Remote Healthcare Services

Telehealth services allow digital nomads to access medical consultations and prescriptions online, ensuring they receive necessary healthcare while traveling.

16. Sustainable Travel Apps

Apps like Ecolife, Good on You, and Happy Cow help nomads make sustainable choices while traveling, from eco-friendly accommodations to ethical dining options.

17. Niche Marketplaces

Specialized marketplaces like Fiverr and Upwork connect digital nomads with freelance opportunities in various fields.

These emerging tools and platforms are the wind in your sails, propelling you forward in your digital nomad journey. Stay curious and open to adopting new technologies that can streamline your work, enhance your travel experience, and keep you connected with a global community of like-minded nomads.

The Impact of Remote Work Trends

The digital nomad lifestyle is closely intertwined with the broader trends of remote work. Let's examine how these trends are shaping the nomadic landscape:

1. Widespread Remote Work Adoption

The COVID-19 pandemic accelerated the adoption of remote work, making it a mainstream practice. More companies now offer remote work options, providing nomads with a wider range of job opportunities.

2. Remote Work Policies

Companies are revising their remote work policies, emphasizing flexibility and results-based performance over traditional office attendance. This shift benefits digital nomads who value location independence.

3. Co-Living and Co-Working Spaces

The demand for co-living and co-working spaces is on the rise. As remote work becomes more prevalent, dedicated spaces for work and accommodation are catering to the needs of digital nomads and remote professionals.

4. Talent Pool Expansion

Companies are tapping into a global talent pool by hiring remote workers from different countries. This trend opens up diverse opportunities for digital nomads with specialized skills.

5. Hybrid Work Models

Hybrid work models, combining remote and in-office work, are becoming common. This flexibility allows digital nomads to collaborate with on-site teams during specific periods.

6. Shift in Priorities

The pandemic has prompted many individuals to reevaluate their priorities. As a result, more people are choosing the nomadic lifestyle for its freedom, work-life balance, and adventure.

7. Remote Work Support Services

Startups and businesses are emerging to cater to the needs of remote workers, offering services like virtual team-building activities, mental health support, and digital nomad insurance.

8. Competitive Salaries

Digital nomads can access job markets with varying salary levels. Some may seek opportunities in countries with lower living costs to maximize their earnings.

9. Changing Work Cultures

Remote work is reshaping traditional work cultures, fostering a greater focus on results and output rather than hours spent in an office.

Preparing for Future Changes

The digital nomad landscape is continually evolving. To thrive in this dynamic environment, consider these strategies for preparing for future changes:

1. Continuous Learning

Stay updated on emerging technologies, tools, and trends in your field of work. Continuous learning will enhance your skillset and keep you competitive.

2. Financial Planning

Build a financial safety net by saving for unexpected expenses or periods of reduced income. Consider investments that generate passive income.

3. Networking

Nurture your professional network by attending virtual events, conferences, and meetups. Building relationships can lead to exciting opportunities and collaborations.

4. Adaptable Mindset

Embrace change with an adaptable mindset. Be open to new opportunities, industries, and locations that may arise in the future.

5. Legal and Tax Advice

Consult with legal and tax professionals who specialize in international issues. They can provide guidance on compliance and tax optimization.

6. Sustainable Practices

Incorporate sustainable practices into your nomadic lifestyle to align with evolving global concerns about environmental responsibility.

7. Diversify Income Streams

Explore multiple income streams, such as freelancing, consulting, online courses, or affiliate marketing, to enhance your financial stability.

8. Health and Wellness

Prioritize your physical and mental well-being by maintaining a healthy lifestyle and accessing healthcare services when needed.

9. Risk Management

Consider insurance options, including health, travel, and liability insurance, to mitigate potential risks and unexpected challenges.

10. Long-Term Goals

Set long-term goals and define your vision for the future. Whether you plan to transition out of nomadism or continue indefinitely, having a clear direction will guide your decisions.

The digital nomad lifestyle is a dynamic adventure that evolves with technology, society, and individual preferences. By staying informed, adaptable, and prepared for change, you can navigate the ever-shifting tides of this exciting journey.

As you embark on your digital nomad voyage, remember that the journey itself is a destination. Embrace the opportunities and challenges that arise, and let the evolving technologies and trends enrich your nomadic experience.

Chapter 19: Reflection and Personal Growth

As we near the end of our adventurous journey through the world of digital nomadism, it's time to turn our gaze inward and explore the profound transformations that can occur within you as a result of this unique lifestyle. In this chapter, we'll delve deep into the introspective realm of reflection and personal growth. We'll uncover how the nomadic life can change you, foster self-discovery, and ultimately lead you to find purpose and fulfillment on your extraordinary journey.

How Digital Nomadism Can Change You

Embarking on the digital nomad journey is like setting sail into uncharted waters. It's not just a change of scenery but a transformation of self. Let's navigate through some of the ways digital nomadism can change you:

1. Adaptability

You'll become a master of adaptability, learning to thrive in ever-changing environments. Navigating unfamiliar cultures, languages, and customs hones your ability to adapt swiftly.

2. Independence

Digital nomadism fosters self-reliance. You'll make decisions independently, from choosing your next destination to managing your finances.

3. Open-Mindedness

Exposure to diverse cultures and perspectives opens your mind to new ideas and ways of thinking. You become more accepting and open-minded.

4. Resilience

Facing unexpected challenges and setbacks while on the road builds resilience. You learn to bounce back from adversity with grace and determination.

5. Resourcefulness

Resourcefulness becomes your ally as you find creative solutions to unforeseen problems, whether it's troubleshooting technical issues or navigating transportation disruptions.

6. Time Management

Balancing work, travel, and personal time sharpens your time management skills. You become adept at prioritizing tasks and setting boundaries.

7. Empathy

Interacting with people from diverse backgrounds cultivates empathy. You'll better understand the struggles and triumphs of others.

8. Minimalism

Living out of a suitcase encourages a minimalist lifestyle. You'll discover that material possessions matter less than experiences and connections.

9. Confidence

Conquering new challenges boosts your self-confidence. You'll realize that you're capable of far more than you once believed.

10. Gratitude

Traveling exposes you to both the beauty and hardships of the world. It fosters a deep sense of gratitude for the opportunities and privileges you have.

11. Cultural Insight

Immersing yourself in different cultures grants you unique insights into the human experience. You'll gain a richer understanding of the world's diversity.

12. Self-Discovery

Digital nomadism offers the gift of self-discovery. Removed from familiar surroundings and routines, you have the opportunity to explore your true self.

Self-Discovery and Personal Development

The digital nomad lifestyle is a fertile ground for self-discovery and personal development. Let's delve deeper into this transformative aspect of nomadic living:

1. Solitude and Reflection

Traveling solo or in small groups allows for moments of solitude and reflection. These quiet moments can lead to profound self-discovery and introspection.

2. Stepping Out of Comfort Zones

Leaving your comfort zone becomes a daily occurrence. Each step taken beyond it is an opportunity for growth.

3. Challenging Assumptions

You'll be confronted with assumptions and biases you may not have been aware of. This self-awareness is a crucial step in personal development.

4. Self-Reliance

Digital nomadism often requires you to rely on your own skills and judgment. This self-reliance can boost your self-esteem and sense of empowerment.

5. Pursuing Passions

Having more control over your time enables you to pursue passions and hobbies that may have been neglected in a traditional lifestyle.

6. Self-Care and Well-Being

Prioritizing self-care and well-being becomes essential. Nurturing your physical and mental health is an integral part of personal development.

7. Building Resilience

Facing challenges head-on builds emotional resilience. You'll learn to bounce back from setbacks with greater fortitude.

8. Learning from Diversity

Interacting with people from various backgrounds fosters cultural intelligence and empathy. You'll gain a broader perspective on humanity.

9. Discovering Values

As you encounter different cultures and lifestyles, you'll refine your values and what truly matters to you.

10. Mindfulness and Presence

Living in the moment becomes a way of life. Mindfulness and presence lead to a deeper appreciation of each experience.

11. Embracing Uncertainty

Embracing uncertainty and change fosters adaptability and flexibility. You'll learn to navigate the unpredictable with grace.

12. Reinventing Identity

The nomadic lifestyle allows for reinventing your identity. You have the freedom to explore different facets of yourself.

Digital nomadism is a transformative journey, not just in the destinations you explore but in the depths of your own being. It's an opportunity for continuous growth and self-evolution.

Finding Purpose and Fulfillment

As you grow and change through your digital nomad experience, you may find yourself on a quest for purpose and fulfillment. Here's how to embark on this rewarding journey:

1. Reflect on Values

Take time to reflect on your core values and what truly matters to you. Consider what gives your life meaning and purpose.

2. Identify Passions

Explore your passions and interests. What activities make you feel alive and engaged? Align your pursuits with your passions.

3. Set Personal Goals

Set personal goals that align with your values and passions. These goals can provide a sense of direction and fulfillment.

4. Cultivate Relationships

Build meaningful connections with fellow nomads and locals. Relationships can be a source of joy and purpose.

5. Give Back

Consider how you can give back to the communities you visit. Engaging in volunteer work or supporting local initiatives can be incredibly fulfilling.

6. Embrace Growth

Welcome personal growth and change as integral parts of your journey. Embrace challenges as opportunities for learning and self-improvement.

7. Seek Balance

Strive for balance in your nomadic lifestyle. Balance work, travel, and personal time to avoid burnout and maintain well-being.

8. Practice Gratitude

Cultivate a daily gratitude practice. Reflecting on the positives in your life can enhance your sense of fulfillment.

9. Live with Intention

Live with intention and purpose. Be mindful of your choices and actions, ensuring they align with your values.

10. Reflect Regularly

Take time for regular introspection and reflection. Journaling or meditation can help you gain clarity on your path.

11. Seek Guidance

Consider seeking guidance from a life coach or mentor. They can provide support and insights on finding purpose and fulfillment.

Your digital nomad journey is not just a physical adventure but a profound exploration of self. Finding purpose and fulfillment is an ongoing quest that can lead you to a deeper sense of contentment and happiness.

As we near the end of our voyage together, take a moment to reflect on how far you've come and the remarkable transformations you've undergone. Whether you've just set sail or have been navigating these nomadic waters for a while, remember that the journey itself is the destination. Your quest for self-discovery, personal growth, purpose, and fulfillment is a testament to the incredible power of the digital nomad lifestyle.

Chapter 20: The Future of Digital Nomadism

As we reach the final chapter of our guide, it's time to cast our gaze toward the horizon and explore the exciting possibilities that lie ahead for digital nomadism. In this chapter, we'll delve into predictions for the future of remote work, the evolving digital nomad community, and how we can inspire and encourage others to embark on this extraordinary journey.

Predictions for the Future of Remote Work

The future of remote work is poised to be nothing short of revolutionary. Let's set our course and explore some predictions for how remote work will continue to shape the world:

1. Hybrid Work Models

Hybrid work models, combining remote and in-office work, will become the norm for many industries. This flexibility offers professionals the best of both worlds—collaborative office environments and the freedom to work remotely when needed.

2. Increased Geographic Flexibility

Remote work will grant employees greater geographic flexibility. Companies will hire talent from diverse locations, reducing the necessity for relocation and allowing professionals to choose where they want to live.

3. Digital Nomad Visas

More countries will introduce digital nomad visas and residency programs, attracting remote workers and freelancers with enticing perks such as tax benefits and streamlined immigration processes.

4. Augmented Reality (AR) and Virtual Reality (VR)

Advancements in AR and VR technology will revolutionize remote collaboration. Teams will be able to meet in virtual spaces, creating a more immersive and engaging remote work experience.

5. Automation and AI

Automation and artificial intelligence will reshape job roles, leading to more opportunities for remote work in fields such as data analysis, content creation, and digital marketing.

6. Sustainable Practices

Remote work can contribute to a reduction in greenhouse gas emissions by reducing the need for daily commuting. Companies will adopt sustainable practices, including carbon offset programs for remote employees.

7. Mental Health Support

As remote work continues to grow, companies will invest in mental health support and resources for remote workers to combat isolation and burnout.

8. Enhanced Connectivity

Global connectivity will improve, ensuring reliable internet access in even the most remote locations, making it easier for digital nomads to work from virtually anywhere.

9. Increased Productivity Tracking

Companies will implement advanced productivity tracking tools to measure remote workers' performance and well-being, with a focus on maintaining a healthy work-life balance.

10. New Industries and Opportunities

The rise of remote work will give rise to new industries and job opportunities, including remote team-building services, remote event planning, and virtual tourism experiences.

11. Lifelong Learning

Lifelong learning will become essential as professionals adapt to evolving technologies and industries. Online courses, certifications, and upskilling will be integral to career growth.

12. Remote Education

Remote education will continue to thrive, offering flexible learning options for students of all ages. Online learning platforms will further democratize access to quality education.

13. Gig Economy Growth

The gig economy will expand, providing remote workers with diverse income opportunities, from freelance writing to virtual assistance.

14. Flexibility in Work Hours

Companies will offer greater flexibility in work hours, allowing employees to design schedules that align with their productivity peaks and personal lives.

15. Remote Management Skills

Leaders will develop remote management skills to effectively lead and motivate remote teams. Training in remote leadership will become a priority.

16. Global Collaboration

Collaboration between global teams will become seamless through advanced digital tools and cultural intelligence training.

17. Distributed Companies

Companies may shift from traditional office-based structures to becoming fully distributed, with teams scattered across the globe.

18. Work-Life Integration

The line between work and personal life will blur as professionals integrate work into their daily routines. This shift will require a greater emphasis on work-life balance and boundary-setting.

19. Travel and Remote Work

Travel and remote work will continue to go hand in hand. More people will embrace the digital nomad lifestyle, leading to the growth of nomad-friendly communities worldwide.

20. Lifelong Nomadism

Some individuals will choose lifelong nomadism, making it a sustainable and fulfilling lifestyle choice.

The Evolving Digital Nomad Community

The digital nomad community is a dynamic and evolving force. Let's set sail into the heart of this vibrant community and explore its future:

1. Digital Nomad Hubs

Nomad hubs in various countries will continue to thrive, offering co-living, co-working, and networking opportunities for nomads.

2. Community-Driven Platforms

Online platforms and communities dedicated to digital nomadism will grow, providing resources, support, and connections for nomads worldwide.

3. Nomadic Families

More families will embrace the digital nomad lifestyle, homeschooling their children while traveling and working remotely.

4. Remote Work Advocacy

Advocacy groups and organizations will emerge to support the rights and well-being of remote workers, including digital nomads.

5. Skill-Sharing Networks

Nomads will engage in skill-sharing networks, where they exchange knowledge and expertise in various fields.

6. Cultural Exchange

The digital nomad community will continue to foster cultural exchange and understanding as individuals from diverse backgrounds come together.

7. Sustainable Nomadism

Sustainability will become a central theme in the digital nomad community, with a focus on eco-conscious travel and responsible tourism.

8. Mentorship and Support

Experienced digital nomads will offer mentorship and support to newcomers, helping them navigate the challenges of the lifestyle.

9. Local Integration

Digital nomads will seek deeper integration into the local communities they visit, participating in volunteer work and cultural events.

10. Nomadism for All Ages

Nomadism will not be limited to a specific age group, with individuals of all ages choosing the lifestyle.

Encouraging Others to Embark on the Journey

As seasoned adventurers in the world of digital nomadism, it's our privilege and duty to inspire and encourage others to embark on this life-changing journey. Here are some ways we can do just that:

1. Share Your Story

Share your own digital nomad story, highlighting the transformative experiences and personal growth you've achieved.

2. Offer Guidance

Provide guidance and practical advice to those considering the nomadic lifestyle, sharing your knowledge on topics like budgeting, travel planning, and remote work.

3. Mentorship

Offer mentorship to aspiring digital nomads, guiding them through the challenges and opportunities of the lifestyle.

4. Promote Remote Work

Advocate for remote work within your professional network and encourage companies to embrace remote work options.

5. Create Resources

Contribute to the digital nomad community by creating resources, such as blogs, podcasts, or YouTube channels, that offer valuable insights and tips.

6. Nomad-Friendly Businesses

Support and promote businesses that cater to digital nomads, from co-living spaces to travel insurance providers.

7. Cultural Sensitivity

Promote cultural sensitivity and responsible tourism among nomads to ensure a positive impact on the communities they visit.

8. Celebrate Diversity

Celebrate the diversity within the digital nomad community, valuing the unique perspectives and backgrounds of its members.

9. Connect and Collaborate

Foster connections and collaborations within the community, organizing meetups, conferences, and networking events.

10. Encourage Inclusivity

Create an inclusive environment where individuals from all backgrounds feel welcome and supported in their digital nomad journey.

11. Pay It Forward

Remember the support and inspiration you received when you began your digital nomad adventure, and pay it forward by extending a helping hand to others.

12. Embrace Challenges

Encourage aspiring nomads to embrace the challenges and uncertainties that come with the lifestyle, assuring them that growth often arises from adversity.

13. Highlight Benefits

Highlight the myriad benefits of digital nomadism, from personal freedom to cultural enrichment, to inspire others to take the leap.

14. Be an Ambassador

Be an ambassador for the digital nomad lifestyle, demonstrating its positive impact on your life and well-being.

15. Encourage Exploration

Encourage individuals to explore new horizons, whether it's through travel, career changes, or personal growth.

End of the Journey

As we conclude our voyage through the captivating world of digital nomadism, remember that this journey is not just about the destinations you explore but the profound transformations that occur within you. It's about the connections you forge, the cultures you embrace, and the limitless horizons of personal growth and fulfillment.

The future of digital nomadism is a tapestry woven with threads of innovation, flexibility, and boundless opportunity. It's a future where individuals from all walks of life can embrace the freedom to work and live on their terms, unburdened by the constraints of geography or tradition.

As we sail into the future, let us do so with open hearts and open minds, ready to embrace the ever-changing landscape of remote work and nomadic living. Let us continue to inspire and support one another, forging a global community bound by a shared passion for exploration and self-discovery.

Whether you're a seasoned nomad, a curious explorer, or someone just setting sail on this incredible journey, know that the digital nomad lifestyle offers a world of possibilities. It's a lifestyle that invites you to dream big, live boldly, and savor every moment of the extraordinary adventure that is life on the road.

So, my fellow travelers, as we bid farewell to this guide and continue our individual odysseys, may your path be filled with wonder, your heart with joy, and your spirit forever untethered. The world is your oyster, and the future of digital nomadism is yours to shape. Bon voyage!

Don't miss out!

Visit the website below and you can sign up to receive emails whenever SERGIO RIJO publishes a new book. There's no charge and no obligation.

https://books2read.com/r/B-A-COYW-ASCOC

BOOKS 2 READ

Connecting independent readers to independent writers.

Also by SERGIO RIJO

Breaking Free: A Guide to Recovery from Narcissistic Abuse
Dreamweaving: The Ultimate Guide to Entering Someone's Dreams
From Isolation to Balance: The Ultimate Guide to Remote Work
Success
The Twin Flames Blueprint: A Guide to Achieving Union and
Embracing the Journey
Insta-Profit: 25 Proven Ways to Monetize Your Instagram Presence
The Awakening: Archangel Michael's Message for a Unified and
Evolved Humanity
Unlock Your Potential: 10 Key Skills for Young People to Have
Success in Life and Career
30 Days of Spiritual Transformation: How to Change Your Life
Through the Power of Spirituality
Brain Overhaul: Upgrading Your Mind for Accelerated Learning and
Success
30 Days to a Richer You: The Millionaire Success Habits That Will
Change Your Life
Separate but Connected: A Guide to Navigating the Twin Flame
Separation Stage
The Rise of AI Income: Using Artificial Intelligence for Financial
Success
Anime Tattoo Design Book: 300+ Designs for Fans and Tattoo
Artists
The Art of Butterfly Tattoos: 300+ Designs to Inspire Your Next
Tattoo

Rose Tattoo Designs: 300+ Designs to Inspire Your Next Tattoo

The Geometric Tattoo Handbook: A Complete Collection of 300+ Designs

Skull Tatoo Designs: Over 300 Tattoo Designs to Inspire You

Soulful: Unlocking the 16 Traits of Advanced Souls

Memory Mastery: The Proven System to Retain Information Effectively

Rise and Shine: A Guide to Kundalini Awakening for the Modern Spiritual Seeker

The Power of Presence: Connecting with Your Higher Self and Living with Purpose

Powerful Techniques for Mastering the Art of Influence: Proven Strategies to Exert Maximum Power and Persuasion

The Art of Remote Viewing: A Step-by-Step Guide to Unlocking Your Psychic Abilities

Money Magnetism: The Art of Attracting Abundance

The Happiness Handbook: A Practical Guide to Finding Joy and Fulfillment

The Smarter You: Proven Ways to Boost Your Intelligence

Appetite Control Strategies: The Secret to Successful Weight Loss

Off The Grid Living: A Comprehensive Guide to Sustainable and Self-Sufficient Living

The Ultimate Guide to Get Your Ex Back: A Step-by-Step Blueprint to Rekindle Love and Heal Your Relationship

Calm and Centered: Overcoming Anxiety and Panic Attacks Naturally

The Power Within: Boosting Self-Esteem and Confidence through Positive Self-Talk and Self-Care Practices

Grateful Living: Transform Your Life with the Power of Gratitude

Procrastination Uncovered: Understanding and Overcoming the Epidemic of Delay

Social Butterfly: Tips and Strategies for Conquering Shyness and Social Anxiety

Living with Purpose: Finding Meaning and Direction in Life
Breaking Free from Self-Sabotage: Overcoming Destructive Patterns
and Achieving Your Goals
Uncovering the Shadows: A Journey through Shadow Work
The Science of Nutrition for Athletes: Understanding the Specific
Nutritional Needs of Athletes for Optimal Performance and Recovery
The Magic of Saying No: How to Establish Boundaries and Take
Charge of Your Life
Connecting with the Divine: Tools and Techniques for Powerful
Prayer
Living in Harmony: The Complete Guide to Permaculture and
Sustainable Living
Angelic Assistance: How to Connect with Your Guardian Angels and
Spirit Guides for Support
Beyond Belief: Unraveling the Psychology of Ghosts and Hauntings
Transform Your Health with Intermittent Fasting: A Comprehensive
Guide to Techniques and Benefits
Discover the Secrets of Lucid Dreaming: How to Use Your Dreams to
Transform Your Life
Existential Crisis: Strategies for Finding Hope and Renewal in Life's
Darkest Moments
The 12 Spiritual Laws of the Universe: A Comprehensive Guide to
Achieving Personal Growth and Spiritual Enlightenment
The 144,000 Lightworkers: Healing and Awakening Humanity to
Save the World
Defying Age: The Ultimate Guide to Living a Long and Healthy Life
Unlocking the Secrets of Astral Projection: Techniques for Successful
Out-of-Body Experiences
Inner Child Healing: The Key to Overcoming Negative Beliefs,
Self-Sabotage, and Unlocking Your True Potential
Raising Your Vibration: A Holistic Guide to Achieving Emotional
and Spiritual Well-being

Psychic Vampires and Empaths: The Ultimate Guide to Protection and Healing with Energy, Crystals, Reiki, and More

Developing Clairvoyance: The Ultimate Guide to Unlocking Your Psychic Gifts and Connecting with the Spiritual World

Mastering Telekinesis: A Step-by-Step Guide to Developing Your Psychokinetic Abilities

Afterlife: Understanding Signs and Communication from Deceased Loved Ones

Navigating Spiritual Depression: Finding Meaning in the Dark Night of the Soul

Journey of the Old Soul: Navigating Life with Empathy, Wisdom, and Purpose

Third Eye Awakening: A Comprehensive Guide to Unlocking Your Inner Vision, Enhancing Intuition, and Activating the Pineal Gland for Spiritual Insight and Heightened Perception

Telepathy Unveiled: A Journey into the Secrets of Sending Telepathic Messages and Psychic Development

44 Letters from God: Divine Guidance for Life's Journey

Mastering Emotional Intelligence: Strategies for Cultivating Self-Awareness, Self-Regulation, and Empathy

The Power of Solitude: Embracing Alone Time for Self-Discovery and Fulfillment

The Ultimate Guide to Beekeeping: Tips and Tricks for Beginners

Akashic Records and Past Lives: Understanding How Past Lives Can Impact Your Present and Future

Mindful Eating for Emotional Freedom: Break the Cycle of Emotional Eating Habits

Stand-Up Comedy: A Guide to Writing and Performing with Confidence

The Art of Budget Travel: Techniques for Saving Money and Maximizing Experiences While Traveling

The Mystic Art of Alchemy: Understanding the Symbolism and Practice of Spiritual Transformation

The Power Within: A Guide to Self-Healing with Energy
Solo Travel: Techniques for Planning and Executing a Successful Solo Trip
The Art of Extreme Budgeting: How to Live on Almost Nothing and Thrive
The Science of Luck: How to Increase Your Odds of Success
The Science of Color: Understanding the Psychology of Color
The Secret Life of the Brain: Exploring the Mysteries and Wonders of Our Most Vital Organ
Listen Up: Unlocking the Secrets of Active Listening
The Power of Self-Love: Transforming Your Life Through Compassion and Acceptance
The Science of Time Travel: Theories and Possibilities Explained
Beyond the Mind's Illusions: Mastering Thought Patterns for Freedom from Suffering
Quantum Light Mastery: Unleashing Infinite Power
The Archetype Code: Unveiling Your True Self
The Empath's Path: Journey to Self-Discovery
Surrender to Freedom: Letting Go for Conscious Living
Metabolism Unleashed: Unlocking Your Body's Hidden Weight Loss Potential
Unburdened: Liberating Your True Self from Emotionally Immature Parents
Healing the Unseen Wounds: Unlocking the Power of Resilience
The Wild Within: Embracing Discomfort for Health, Growth, and Happiness
Beyond the Ordinary: Unleashing Your Supernatural Potential
The Pendulum Power Guide: Unleash Magic, Healing, and Divination in Your Life
Beyond the Veil: Unleashing Your Spiritual Mediumship
Awakening the Shaman Within: Unveiling the Mysteries of Ancient Wisdom
The Sacred Geometry Guidebook: Illuminating the Power of Patterns

Law of Attraction Mastery: Unleashing Your Manifestation Power for Abundance and Fulfillment

Cosmic Harmony: A Guide to Unraveling Synchronicities, Signs, and Spiritual Awakening for a Fulfilling Life

Journey to the Ancestral Realms: Unveiling the Secrets of Spirit Guides

Whispers of Eternity: Exploring the Mysteries of Death, Reincarnation, and the Afterlife

Starseed Secrets: Unveiling Your Cosmic DNA

The Joyful Mindset Makeover: Transform Your Life Through Positive Emotions

Mastering Emotional Resilience: Thriving in the Face of Challenges

Uncomplicate: Mastering Happiness and Success Through Simplicity

Success Habits: Unveiling the Blueprint to Achievement and Fulfillment

Unleash Your Creative Genius: Tapping into Your Innate Imagination and Innovation

Beyond Materialism: Finding Meaning and Happiness in a Consumerist World

Redefining Success: Creating a Life Aligned with Your Values and Purpose

Living Beyond Limits: Unleashing Your Full Potential through Spiritual Laws

The Enlightened Mindset: Cultivating Spiritual Awareness in Everyday Life

The Path to Inner Harmony: Balancing Spiritual Enlightenment and Modern Living

Empowered Intuition: A Guide to Navigating Life through Spiritual Insight

Manifesting Miracles: Activating Spiritual Laws to Create Your Dream Life

Sacred Relationships: Nurturing Connections through Spiritual Laws

The Soulful Entrepreneur: Integrating Spiritual Laws into Business Success

Interpreting the Signs: A Guide to Understanding Messages from the Spirit World

Mystical Synchronicities: Exploring the Divine Order in Everyday Life

The Minimalist Vegan: How to Live a More Ethical, Eco-Friendly, and Healthier Life

Stars Aligned: Unveiling the Secrets of Zodiac Compatibility

The Love Language: How to Speak Your Partner's Love Language and Build a Deeper Connection

The Power of Focus: How to Stay Focused on Your Goals and Achieve Success

How to Become a Digital Nomad: Your Roadmap to Location Independence

The Leadership Challenge: How to Keep Your People Engaged and Inspired

About the Author

Join me on an adventure through captivating stories! I'm Sergio Rijo, a passionate writer with 20 years of experience in crafting books across genres. Let's explore new worlds together and get hooked from start to finish.

Printed by Libri Plureos GmbH in Hamburg, Germany